Maz to Yaz to Amazin':
Baseball's Spectacular 1960s

About the Author

Thad Mumau has written professionally for 50 years, working with a daily newspaper much of that time and contributing to several magazines. As a sports writer, he covered numerous Atlantic Coast Conference and NCAA basketball tournaments, including several Final Fours.

Maz to Yaz to Amazin' is his eighth book and his fourth about baseball. Among the others is the very first biography written about Hall of Fame college basketball coach Dean Smith.

Mumau has spent his life in Fayetteville, North Carolina. He and his wife, Dahlia, have two daughters.

Here are Thad's other books:

The Dean Smith Story: More Than a Coach
Go Wolfpack: North Carolina State football
Dean Smith: A Biography
An Indian Summer: The 1957 Milwaukee Braves, Champions of Baseball
When the Grass Turns Green: Cherished Baseball Memories of a North Carolina Sportswriter
Conversations with Dean Smith
Had 'em All the Way: the 1960 Pittsburgh Pirates

Maz to Yaz to Amazin':
Baseball's Spectacular 1960s

By
Thad Mumau

SUMMER
GAME
BOOKS

ISBN: 978-1-938545-85-6 (print)
ISBN: 978-1-938545-86-3 (ebook)

For information about permission, bulk purchases, or additional distribution, write to

Summer Game Books
P. O. Box 818
South Orange, NJ 07079
or contact the publisher at www.summergamebooks.com

Dedication

For Dahlia, as always, with love.

Acknowledgments

My love of baseball goes back to my dad. He taught me about the game and how it should be played. There was no instruction, just conversation while we played catch, listened to ball games on the radio, and watched our local minor league team.

Dad took pleasure in seeing someone hit the cutoff man, back up a throw, lay down a bunt, hit the inside corner of second base to shorten the path to third . . . the fundamentals. I learned those from him, along with an appreciation for a beautiful sport.

He was generous with his patience and time, so much of it spent with me after he had worked unbelievably hard all day. He always had time for his son and daughter and wife. Obviously, the most important lessons I learned from him were not about a game.

My mother was always my inspiration. An amazing athlete, she battled an unbeatable illness most of her life, displaying relentless courage and determination to never give up.

My sister Judy used to throw me batting practice with a plastic ball, and she continues to pull for me in all I do.

Dahlia, my wife, is the reason for anything I accomplish. I could fill a page with glowing adjectives, but the fact that she is the best person I have ever known says everything.

Tom Suiter was my content cop for *Maz to Yaz to Amazin'*. Like me, he grew up filled with the excitement of 1960s baseball. He has tremendous recall of the teams and players from that decade, and as he read what I wrote, he offered numerous suggestions that made this book better.

Tom is a good friend and an encourager, and he provided me with a constant boost.

Thanks to all these wonderful people, along with my daughters, Erika and Laura.

Contents

Introduction

My earliest memories of baseball are being huddled next to a radio with my dad, listening to the pitiful Pirates over KDKA in Pittsburgh.

Then there was the Game of the Day on the radio, which gave me a taste of the rest of the baseball world. I used to run an extension cord out the kitchen window so I could listen to the games while I worked in the yard.

I learned two lessons quickly: The Pittsburgh Pirates were always awful and the World Series was an annual duel of Yankees and Dodgers.

Things began to change in the late 1950s, and I began to learn there was much more to baseball. First, the Pirates won!—and that was followed by what I still think is the most exciting decade in baseball history—the incredible 1960s. Packed with star players, thrilling pennant races, and great drama and change, the decade was also loaded with charm and intrigue—its own distinctive personality. New champions, new teams, new rules, and new stars.

I digested every word about baseball in *Sport Magazine* and the *Sporting News*, read every article and box score I could get my hands on, and continued to stay glued to the radio. I couldn't get enough of the game and its players.

Our family didn't have a TV for quite a while; newspaper and magazine photos of major league players provided the only visuals of the men who were bigger than life to me. In some ways, that romantic vision of the decade never changed inside of me.

Nellie Fox with a chaw so big it left stretch marks on his jaw. Rocky Colavito pointing his menacing bat at the pitcher. Willie Mays running out from under his hat. An aging Warren Spahn, forever frozen by a camera in the middle of that classic windup.

Baseball in the 1960s is like a long series of vivid snapshots and glittering stat sheets of the players who were the heroes of me and thousands of other fans.

Nostalgia is the very nature of baseball. The game's foundation is a rich, intertwined history and our memories of it, and my favorite baseball memories are from the 60s. The 1960s was a decade of fantastic feats by both players and teams and myriad changes on the field and off that altered the landscape of the game forever.

There was a whole lot going on beyond baseball in the nation and the world during that time—social and political change that affected and still affects us individually and collectively. Some of that upheaval spilled into the game, and some of the game's changes spilled into our culture in fascinating ways.

But that isn't what this book is about. This book is pure baseball. My goal is to share the thrills and good feelings the game gave me and all its fans over the decade that was truly the pinnacle of the game.

Some of the stories of the teams and players will be familiar to fans; other stories will be not so well known. But all readers are sure to be wowed by the sheer number of great players, great plays, and great games that were packed into the decade. It's easy to forget a Marichal when you have a Koufax, a Kaline when you have a Clemente, a Brooks when you have a Frank.

There's Gibby and Willie and Denny and Hank. But don't forget Diamond Jim, the Harmonica Man, and old Barney, too. Fireballers and knuckleballers, sluggers and speedsters, Cooperstown royalty and mere serfs come and gone like a flash. Pennant races, triple crowns, historic homers, and unmatched pitching excellence.

This book captures the majesty of 1960s baseball, and attempts to rekindle some of the magic of the game during those times, when the stars and drama of baseball made lifelong fans of so many of us.

Author's Note

Work for this book began more than a decade ago. One-on-one, face-to-face interviews with players were done while I was a full-time sports writer for *The Fayetteville Observer*, the newspaper in my North Carolina home town. Assignments occasionally afforded me the opportunity to talk with players while covering games. Several interviews, particularly those from recent years, were done by telephone, as part of the development of the content of the book.

Chapter 1

Baseball at Its Best

Roberto Clemente unleashes one of his rocket throws, the force of his follow-through lifting his feet off the ground. **Maury Wills** slides into second, dirt flying, as he swipes yet another base. **Sandy Koufax** points his right leg into the air, about to deliver one more jackhammer curve or jet-propelled fastball.

Carl Yastrzemski, looking like a racquetball champion, plays a carom perfectly off the Green Monster. Smooth as fresh cream, **Brooks Robinson** makes a patented backhand stab behind third base.

Bob Gibson kicks at the rubber and stares defiantly at a batter, daring him to dig in. **Frank Robinson**, unruffled by a knockdown pitch, glares toward the mound and resumes his stance right on top of the plate.

Henry Aaron eases into the batter's box, so relaxed he could be playing in a picnic softball game, flicks his lethal wrists, and sends yet another drive soaring over the fence.

Ever terrific, **Tom Seaver** stages an on-the-job clinic on pitching mechanics as he explodes out of his compact delivery and throws strike after strike.

Smoky Burgess and **Jerry Lynch** and **Manny Mota** stretch cold muscles when called upon to climb off the bench and hit late in a close game. Defying odds and the nature of the human body, they once again deliver in the pinch. They are just as important in the scheme of things as the everyday guys, yet only a line in the box score. Deluxe in the clutch.

Same with the second-class citizens in the bullpen. At least, that was their plight throughout baseball history. Until new strategies and a new statistic changed all that.

The 1960s began with 16 teams and two leagues that each sent a pennant winner to the World Series. The decade concluded with 24 teams, with two expansions increasing the total by 50 percent.

Divisional alignment signaled a new era, with post-season playoffs in both leagues preceding the Fall Classic. The Series was no longer simply a matchup of the teams with the best record in the National and American leagues.

Major League Baseball powers-that-be decided there was too much offense, so the strike zone was expanded early in the 1960s. Then fans complained that there wasn't enough scoring, hence the lowering of the pitcher's mound and raising of the run count late in the decade.

The mighty, they did fall, the New York Yankees plummeting from dynasty to disaster. Their method of destruction—pummeling opponents into submission—was overshadowed by opponents' balance of pitching and hitting, and by offenses spiced with speed.

The Los Angeles Dodgers and St. Louis Cardinals used that formula to win four World Series titles between them in the 1960s.

Integration of the majors was old news by the dawning of the decade, and as it progressed, the number of African American All-Star players grew substantially.

Baseball players looked and sounded different. Some wore their hair longer and grew mustaches and mutton chop sideburns. Some began voicing their opinions and feelings, with two writing books that dared to reveal fraternity secrets.

The decade was remarkable for so many reasons. Fifty-four players who played during the 1960s have plaques in Cooperstown. That is the most of any decade. Some of the most glorious all-time baseball names finished out their careers during the '60s.

A pair of monumental home runs ushered in the 1960s, and both have been talked and written about ever since. One of the blasts won a World Series. The other was the perfect swan song.

Bill Mazeroski's homer off **Ralph Terry** was the first to end a World Series, what is now called a "walk-off," giving the Pittsburgh Pirates victory over the New York Yankees. Many people think it was the most dramatic finish ever to a championship in any sport.

Mazeroski had hit only 11 homers during the 1960 regular season. He was a .260 lifetime hitter who is in the Hall of Fame because of extraordinary defensive ability, punctuated by his unparalleled skill at turning the double play.

The second momentous home run was hit by **Ted Williams** in his last major league at-bat. Sure, it was the kind of thing dreams are made of, but with the Splendid Splinter, it was the kind of theatrics folks expected.

Williams was one of several famous names that were no longer on the major league scene by the time 1970 rolled around, and others were in different uniforms as a result of trades.

The Kid—that was Williams' favorite nickname for himself—was the first of 15 Hall of Fame players to leave baseball during the 1960s, and he bowed out in typically splendid fashion.

It was a damp day on September 28, 1960, in Fenway Park, when he belted a pitch from Baltimore right-hander **Jack Fisher** through heavy air and into the Red Sox's bullpen in right-center field.

It was career home run number 521 for the man known at different times as The Kid, Teddy Ballgame, and the Thumper, in addition to the Splendid Splinter. Twenty others have homered in their final major league trip to the plate, but none of them has a plaque in Cooperstown.

Williams was born 30 years too soon. Imagine him as a designated hitter. He would have been perfect. In the infant years of the DH, some men who were given that job complained that it was difficult to keep their minds on the game when not playing defense and being totally involved.

Williams would never have seen that as a problem. He was always thinking about hitting anyway, always mentally critiquing his last at-bat and planning for his next one. Who knows, he may have batted .400 multiple times if his sole responsibility was his favorite position: Hitter.

It was 77 years ago that Williams batted .406, and no one has hit .400 since. He was 23 years old when his amazing 1941 season ended. What may be more astounding is that he was 39 when he batted .388. Just five more hits would have put him at .400 in 1957. He won the American League batting title that year and repeated in 1958. His career numbers include a .344 batting average, a .634 slugging percentage, and another-worldly .482 on-base percentage.

Branch Rickey, in a lengthy and professorial 1954 article in *Life* magazine that was way ahead of its time, explained why on-base percentage is more important than batting average. Williams stacked 12 seasons with the best AL on-base percentage on top of six batting titles.

He was 42 years old when he trotted around the bases for the last time in his trademark fashion, head down and moving as if in a hurry to escape the crowd's adoration.

In his farewell season, Williams batted .316, with 29 home runs and respective .451 and .645 on-base and slugging percentages. It was the second-lowest batting average in Williams' 19 major league seasons. The abomination, .254, had come in 1959 and was a big reason he came back to play one more year.

And he departed as he started.

While Williams knew the ideal time to quit, **Warren Spahn** did not. At least that is what we surmise when using the standard formula on when to retire from a sport. The idea, most would agree, is for an athlete to leave before his skills do—before he embarrasses himself and replaces memories of greatness with visions of mediocrity or worse. Based on that, Spahn hung around baseball too long.

He had a 6–13 won-loss record in 1964, with an obese earned run average. He pitched fewer than 245 innings for the first time in 18 years and managed just four complete games after averaging 21 for 17 years. But even with those numbers, and perhaps a more telling 44 (birthdays), Spahn pitched on.

Milwaukee sold him to the New York Mets following the '64 season, and the Mets released the old left-hander in July after he had gone 4–12. The Giants signed him, and although Spahn pitched creditably (3–4, 3.39), they released him when the season was done.

He still did not quit. Spahn pitched in the Mexican League in 1966 and in the Pacific Coast League in '67. Criticized for sticking around too long, he said, "I don't care what the public thinks. I'm pitching because I enjoy pitching."

When there was nowhere else he could continue doing that, he retired at the age of 46. "I didn't quit," Spahn said. "Baseball retired me." There is something admirable about a man playing baseball because he loves it, with no fear or concern of tarnishing his image.

It was hard for Spahn to accept that he was finished. Looking at his 1963 season, it is easy to understand why he felt that way.

At the age of 42, he threw 22 complete games, worked 259.2 innings, went 23–7, pitched seven shutouts, and posted a 2.60 earned run average.

That was also the year Spahn was involved in perhaps the greatest pitching duel ever.

On July 2, 1963, the Braves' southpaw and the Giants' **Juan Marichal** were the starting pitchers at Candlestick Park. Spahn was 42 years old, Marichal 25. Both were bound for the Hall of Fame.

Juan Marichal had pinpoint control and a wide repetoire of pitches. He broke into the majors with a 2-hit shutout. (National Baseball Hall of Fame and Museum)

Both pitched shutouts through nine innings. And they both continued. One inning after another. One zero after another. When it was suggested to Marichal that maybe he should call it a night, he said, "There's no way I'm coming out as long as that old man keeps pitching."

Marichal, the high-kicking, hard-throwing right-hander, threw 227 pitches. Spahn, the left-hander with the hawk nose and slick pickoff move, threw 201.

Willie Mays drove No. 201 far into the night, ending the dual marathon pitching performance. It had lasted 16 innings and more than four hours.

No wonder Spahnie thought he could keep going.

SANDY KOUFAX KNEW he could not, but his retirement had nothing to do with diminishing skills. In fact, Koufax was in his prime when he called it quits at the tender age of 30.

The Dodgers' left-hander was nothing special until 1963. Entering that season, his record over eight years was 68–60. He always had plenty of stuff, but did not throw enough of it for strikes.

From 1958–60, he averaged more than five walks per nine innings. Gradually improving, Koufax produced a sparkling walks-per-nine of 1.68 in '63 and kept the number at 2.1 and less his final three seasons.

The result was that he became THE Sandy Koufax, aka sheer dominance, as reflected by numbers that were other-worldly.

The only pitcher to retire the year after winning the Cy Young Award, Koufax announced in November of 1966, a month before his 31st birthday, that his severely arthritic left elbow was forcing him to stop playing. His arm had been in terrible pain for three seasons and was said by one doctor to resemble the arm of a 90-year-old man.

Over his last 10 seasons, hitters batted just .203 against Koufax. For his final four seasons, he won 97 games, lost just 27, never had an earned run average higher than 2.04, and struck out 1,228 in 1,192.2 innings.

Koufax was a unanimous Cy Young Award winner in 1963, '65, and '66 and was the National League MVP in '63, finishing second in that balloting in '65 and '66.

Spahn's 363 wins are the most by any left-hander in baseball history and were accumulated in 21 seasons. Koufax played 12, and he was overpowering most of the last five. He became the youngest player (at 36 years and 21 days) elected to the Baseball Hall of Fame.

While Spahn was the winningest lefty and Koufax was arguably the greatest, **Whitey Ford** was the most efficient. His career winning percentage of .690 is fourth on the all-time list (behind right-handers Spud Chandler, Pedro Martinez, and Dave Foutz, in that order). Casey Stengel's money pitcher compiled a 236–106 record over 16 seasons, with a 2.75 career earned run average.

The Yankees and their longtime World Series rivals, the Dodgers, had grown old together. By the end of the 1960s, the playing days were over for all of the key members of those teams that met in six Fall Classics over a 10-year period (1947–56).

Ford retired following the 1967 season after winning two games each of his last two years. **Mickey Mantle** would quit the next year. **Yogi Berra**, who appeared in four games as a player-coach with the New York Mets in 1965, had been released by the Yankees after the 1963 season. **Moose Skowron** was gone by then, and so was **Hank Bauer**, both traded away.

The Dodgers, who moved from Brooklyn to Los Angeles after the 1957 season, had basically rebuilt their team to fit their new home. Roger Kahn's Boys of Summer were replaced by young dazzlers, while a few of the Old Faithful were recycled before they, and the others who remained on the L.A. roster, gradually departed baseball.

The Yankees, of course, stayed in New York but they would never seem as glamorous.

In addition to the marquee names, there were other players who retired in the 1960s after helping the Dodgers and Yankees make regular treks to the World Series in the late 1940s and into the 1950s.

Best-known from the Yankees were Bobby Richardson, Gil McDougald, Elston Howard, Bob Turley, and Don Larsen.

And, of course, there was the Old Perfessor. **Casey Stengel** managed his last game in 1965. He had been "retired" by the Yankees following the 1960 season, prompting Casey to say, "I'll never make the mistake of turning 70 again."

In his 12 years as the Yanks' skipper, they won 10 American League pennants and seven World Series titles, including five in a row. Stengel managed the Mets from their inception in 1962 until the middle of the '65 season, when he resigned, three months to the day after getting win No. 3,000 as a manager.

One year after he left baseball, Stengel was elected to the Baseball Hall of Fame.

Stan Musial's last season was 1963. The left-handed hitter with the corkscrew stance and silky-smooth swing was the National League's answer to Williams in consistency and hitting prowess. Musial, a three-time MVP, won seven batting titles.

He strung together one of the most impressive hitting-for-power-and-average streaks in major league history. From 1943–54 (he was in the military service in 1945), Stan the Man averaged more than 200 hits and

25 home runs per season. During that span, he batted as high as .376 and .365, falling below .330 only once.

Fifteen Hall of Famers closed out their playing careers in the 1960s. Most notable were Musial, Williams, Mantle, Berra, Ford, Koufax, **Don Drysdale**, **Duke Snider**, and Spahn. The others were **Eddie Mathews**, **Richie Ashburn**, **Robin Roberts**, **Nellie Fox**, **Red Schoendienst**, and **Early Wynn**.

The saddest departure of the decade was made by **Herb Score**, the southpaw who flashed Koufax-like stuff before Koufax. Score struck out 508 batters in 476.2 innings in his first two seasons, earning the 1955 Rookie of the Year award and winning 20 games for Cleveland the next season.

The Indians had themselves a 23-year-old ace, but not for long. The infamous line drive off the bat of the Yankees' Gil McDougald struck Score in the right eye in May of 1957, and he was never the same. He won 19 games over parts of seven frustrating years before retiring four games into the 1962 season.

NOBODY COULD REMEMBER seeing someone sprint to first base after drawing a walk. **Pete Rose** made a habit of doing that. He didn't so much slide head-first into bases; he belly-flopped. In the beginning, he wore a flat top and had a jutting chin to go with it.

Rose had a cocky air about him. He was sure he could play this game. And, boy, could he. A switch-hitter, he slapped singles and doubles all over the lot. He ran hard, played hard.

An incessant hustler, he turned many a single into a two-bagger, and he ran out everything. Sometimes it paid off with an infield single, sometimes it got him a double on a pop fly that would have had many hitters trotting disgustedly toward first.

Charlie Hustle was the perfect nickname.

On April 8, 1963, six days before his 22nd birthday, Rose was in Cincinnati's opening-day lineup at Crosley Field. Batting second and playing second base, he went 0-for-3 with a walk against Pittsburgh.

Rose struggled early and finished fast to end at .273 with 101 runs scored. He batted .269 his second year. After that, he hit .301 or higher nine straight years and 14 of the next 15.

He had 200 or more hits 10 times, won back-to-back batting titles, and was an MVP. He has more hits than anyone in baseball history, even more than Ty Cobb.

Rose is famous for that. And for gambling on baseball. And for not being in the Hall of Fame. Perhaps as notable as anything is that Charlie Hustle was the ring leader of the steamrolling Big Red Machine. He set the table for **Sparky Anderson's** pile drivers, men like **Johnny Bench, Tony Perez**, and **George Foster**.

They debuted in the 1960s as well.

SO DID **JOE MORGAN**. He was the ideal two hitter, with Rose leading off. Called "Little Joe" early in his career because of his 5-foot-7 stature, he was big in the power department and was also very fast.

Morgan was a real thorn in the side of a pitcher. Drawing more than 100 walks eight seasons, he would not swing at bad pitches, and when he got a good one, he could send it over the fence.

Turning walks into doubles was Morgan's specialty as he had an 81 percent stolen base success rate over his 22-year career. He finished with 268 home runs, 689 steals, and 1,650 runs scored.

Like Rose, Morgan broke into the big leagues in 1963 when he got into a handful of games with Houston. He became a regular two years later and joined the Cincinnati Reds in 1972.

Chapter 2

1960: "Everyman's" Pirates

The 1960 Pittsburgh Pirates were Everyman's Team.

Dick Groat was the leader of a Pirates team that won the National League pennant and the World Series without a single hitter having a monster year.

No Pirate drove in as many as 100 runs, and **Dick Stuart** was the team home run leader with 23. Pittsburgh's championship season was truly a team effort. Groat elaborated:

"What we accomplished in 1960 was a total team effort. You hear people saying that, and sometimes there are a couple of guys who have real big years and carry the club practically the entire season. With us, it was literally a different guy every day.

"There wasn't any question that Bobby Clemente was the most talented player on the team. And he had a big year for us. But everybody on that team did things that contributed to our winning the National League pennant.

"We picked each other up," noted Groat with pride. "Two or three of us might be in a slump, and here was a guy coming off the bench with a big hit or driving in big runs. Or somebody who had not been hitting much got hot when some of us weren't.

"The '60 Pirates knew how to play baseball. We knew how to produce a run; we could scramble. We did all the little things. Somebody would hit a ground ball to the right side and move a runner over to third. Then we'd get a fly ball, and there . . . we had a run.

"One thing people didn't realize," he pointed out, "was that we were an excellent base running team. No, we did not have a lot of speed, and we didn't steal a lot of bases. But there is so much more to base running.

"We seldom made a base running blunder. We went from first to third on a single. We got good leads so we could do that and so we could score from second on a hit. We could bunt, and we had hitters who used the whole field rather than trying to pull the ball all the time and thinking about home runs.

"Yes sir, the 1960 Pittsburgh Pirates were a team in every sense of the word."

When the 1960 World Series concluded, Mickey Mantle sat at his locker in the Yankees' dressing room and cried. He said the reason for his tears was that he knew his team was better than the Pirates.

After all, New York had more than doubled Pittsburgh's run total over the seven games, outscoring the Bucs, 55–27, with the Yanks' wins coming in lopsided fashion: 16–3, 10–0, and 12–0.

But as Groat said, the Pirates found a way to win all season, and they were champions because they did that in the four Series games that were close.

THERE WERE FEWER than 14,000 fans in Candlestick Park on July 19, 1960, when San Francisco right-hander Juan Marichal made his major league debut against the visiting Philadelphia Phillies.

It took only two hours and seven minutes to play the game, which Marichal owned. He struck out a dozen Phillies, walked one, and allowed one hit, a two-out single by pinch-hitter Clay Dalrymple in the eighth inning. The Giants won, 2–0.

Marichal would go on to throw 51 more shutouts, become a six-time 20-game winner, and post a 2.69 earned run average in a career that would earn him the nickname "Dominican Dandy," as well as a plaque in Cooperstown.

"He had four or five pitches, all with different speeds," said **George Altman**, an outfielder who enjoyed back-to-back outstanding '60s seasons with the Cubs.

"Marichal kept hitters off balance; he could tie you up in knots. Definitely a guy I had rather not face."

CARROLL HARDY was a lightweight hitter who went to bat for three of baseball's authentic offensive heavyweights, including two Hall of Famers.

The journeyman outfielder played for four teams over eight big league seasons. Hardy's career batting average was .225, with his best year 1962 when he hit eight homers and drove in 36 runs for the Boston Red Sox.

On September 20 of 1960, Hardy became the only man to ever pinch hit for Ted Williams. It happened in Baltimore when Williams fouled the ball off his foot in the first inning.

Hardy, batting against **Hal "Skinny" Brown** with one out and **Willie Tasby** on first base, lined into a double play. Brown caught the ball and doubled Tasby off first to end the inning.

Eight days later in Boston, with the Orioles again providing the opposition, Williams slugged a home run in his final career at-bat. That happened in the bottom of the eighth inning.

Williams figured he was

Carroll Hardy is the only player ever to pinch hit for Ted Williams. He also pinch hit for Carl Yastrzemski and Roger Maris.

done for the day, but Red Sox manager Mike Higgins sent him out to left field in the top of the ninth. As soon as he arrived at his spot, Williams looked up and saw Hardy replacing him.

"They booed me all the way out and cheered Ted all the way in," Hardy recalled.

On May 31, 1961, in Boston, Hardy batted for rookie Carl Yastrzemski. The Red Sox were trailing the Yankees, 7–4, in the bottom of the eighth when Hardy pinch hit for Yaz leading off the inning.

Batting against lefty **Luis Arroyo**, Hardy beat out a bunt for a single and later came around to score. He knocked in a run in the ninth inning with a ground ball as New York nipped Boston, 7–6.

Hardy thus became the only player ever to pinch hit for two members of the Hall of Fame.

He also had one other notable pinch-hit appearance. Triple notable. This took place in the first game of a doubleheader in Cleveland (vs. Chicago) on May 18, 1958, Hardy's 25th birthday.

It was the bottom of the eleventh inning, score tied 4–4, and the Indians had two runners on base.

Southpaw **Billy Pierce** was on the mound for the White Sox, and **Roger Maris**, a left-handed batter, was due. Indians manager **Bobby Bragan** sent the right-handed hitting Hardy up instead, and he belted a pitch over the left-field fence for a three-run, game-winning pinch home run.

Maris would one day be mentioned in the same breath with Babe Ruth. Hardy got a lot of mileage out of those three pinch-hit at-bats.

GEORGE CROWE SET A MAJOR LEAGUE RECORD in May of 1960 when he hit a pinch hit home run off Milwaukee's **Don McMahon** in a 5–2 St. Louis win.

It was the eleventh pinch homer of his career, and at the time, that was the most in baseball history.

Crowe, who was named the first Mr. Basketball in Indiana, was a graduate of the University of Indianapolis. He played in the National Basketball League, which preceded the National Basketball Association.

He played baseball for the New York Black Yankees of the Negro National League before signing with the Boston Braves. Crowe is believed to be the only athlete to compete against **Jackie Robinson** professionally in both baseball and basketball.

An outstanding hitter, he would probably have been a regular for many big league teams if not for the apprehension by team executives of having too many African American players on the field at the same time.

Crowe showed what he could do as an everyday player in 1957 when **Ted Kluszewski**, Cincinnati's starting first baseman, hurt his back. Crowe played 120 games at first for the Redlegs, clouted 31 home runs, and drove in 92 runs.

It was the only time in his nine-year career that he went to bat more than 345 times in a season. Crowe was known mainly for his ability to come off the bench and produce in the clutch. He hit 14 career pinch homers.

THE YANKEES WERE THE POWER poster boys of the 1950s, when they played in eight Fall Classics and won six of them, each of the world championships preceded by regular seasons in which New York either slammed the most or second-most home runs in the American League.

Muscle was the mantra for New York during that decade and on into the next. Nothing wrong with that except, as the Pirates proved, it does not guarantee winning best-of-seven series.

The Yanks began the 1960s with five straight Series appearances, winning it all in 1961 and '62, when they placed first and second, respectively, in American League homers.

National League teams then took five of the last seven World Series titles of the decade, with the Los Angeles Dodgers and St. Louis Cardinals winning two apiece, both of those teams making speed a featured weapon.

"Finding a way to win" was echoed in the 1960s by other clubs that did not necessarily flex the most muscles. The two most prodigious home run hitters of the decade played on teams that accomplished very little.

Harmon Killebrew led all of baseball with 393 home runs and added 1,013 RBIs during the decade, while his Washington Senators/Minnesota Twins won just one American League pennant (1965) in his 22-year major league career.

Hank Aaron led the 1960s with 1,107 runs batted in and was second with 375 homers, and his Milwaukee/Atlanta Braves did not reach a World Series during the decade. He played in two during his 23 years in the big leagues, both in the '50s.

Mazeroski's historic homer made a World Series winner of a team that was not laden with power. The 1960 Pirates, who ranked sixth among eight National League teams in home runs, led the league in singles and doubles and in the most-important runs scored column.

The four American League World Series champs in the decade all finished first or second in the league in home runs. Whereas power was the name of the game for AL clubs that won championships during the 1960s, the opposite was true for the National League teams that won Series titles.

None of the six 60's NL world champs placed in the top three in the league in homers, and five of the six finished sixth or lower. The trend was started by the 1959 Dodgers, whose home run total was fifth among the eight National League teams.

That broke a string of 16 consecutive years the World Series winner had finished in the top three in home runs in its league.

STARTING IN 1960—**Steve Barber, Julian Javier, Tommy Davis, Willie Davis**, Juan Marichal, Clay Dalrymple, **Ray Sadecki, Phil Regan, Ron Santo, Frank Howard, Ron Hansen, Jim Kaat**.

Among the rookies was Santo, the beloved Cubs third baseman and broadcaster who was inducted into the Hall of Fame, sadly, not until after he had passed away.

Santo hit 25 or more home runs eight straight years, slugging 342 in his 15-year career. He was an outstanding fielder with great range and a nine-time All-Star.

Howard and Hansen were Rookies of the Year.

Howard, the 6-foot-7, 255-pound masher known as "Hondo," hit 382 home runs in a career that spanned 16 seasons, most of it with the Dodgers and Senators. He clouted 44, 48, and 48 homers in 1968, '69, and '70 for Washington. The 44 in 1968—the Year of the Pitcher—was especially impressive as only two other American Leaguers reached 30 that season, Willie Horton (36) and Ken "Hawk" Harrelson (35).

Regan, nicknamed "The Vulture" for his knack of picking up victories out of the bullpen, was a starting pitcher when he came up with Detroit. When the Dodgers acquired him, they used him almost exclusively in relief.

In 1966, Regan's first season with Los Angeles, he went 14–1 with a 1.62 and a National League-leading 21 saves. Two years later, he finished 62 of 73 games in which he appeared.

"Kitty" Kaat pitched 25 years in the major leagues and won 283 games, one less than Ferguson Jenkins and four fewer than Bert Blyleven. Kaat is not in the Hall of Fame; the other two are.

The left-hander was a three-time 20-game winner, including 1966 when he won 25 for the Minnesota Twins. He also won an amazing 16 Gold Gloves and batted a solid (for a pitcher) .185 for his career, with 16 home runs.

ENDING IN 1960—Ted Williams, **Don Newcombe, Bobby Thomson, Carl Furillo, Al Dark, Whitey Lockman, Sandy Amoros, Mickey Vernon, Ray Boone**, Gil McDougald.

Thomson, of course, is an icon. Hitting the Shot Heard 'Round the World made him forever synonymous with the word clutch. He clouted 20 or more home runs eight times and drove in over 100 runs three seasons. Slugging 264 homers, he never struck out more than 78 times in a season.

Vernon won two batting titles with the old Washington Senators and had over 200 hits both years. He had 490 career doubles, 51 in 1946 when he batted .353. The lefty first baseman played 22 years.

Boone is the father of defensive catching standout Bob Boone and the granddaddy of Bret and Aaron Boone. All major leaguers. In the 1950s, Ray was a heck of a player himself. He hit at least 20 home runs five times and twice had over 100 RBIs.

McDougald was a vital cog in the New York Yankees' run to glory that produced eight American League pennants from 1951–60, when he played for the club.

The infielder was Mr. Dependable, playing more than 100 games in separate seasons at second base, shortstop, and third base. A .276 lifetime hitter, McDougald hit seven home runs and had 24 RBIs in eight World Series, five of which the Yankees won. He placed fifth in the 1957 American League MVP voting.

LAST PITCH OF 1960 SEASON—from Yankees pitcher Ralph Terry to Bill Mazeroski. The Pittsburgh second baseman hit it over the left-center field wall at Forbes Field, giving the Pirates a 10–9 win in Game Seven of the World Series.

Chapter 3

Let's Make a Deal

Trades are a huge and entertaining part of baseball, whether they add drama at the in-season deadline or spice to the off-season. In fact, the discussion of prospective deals, along with the actual transactions themselves, warm fans' winters so much that the collective activity is known as the Hot Stove League.

There were some zany deals pulled off in the 1960s, the most unusual being Frank "Trader" Lane's even-up swap of managers. Nothing Lane did was too shocking. Whereas Leo Durocher allegedly claimed he'd have a knock-down pitch thrown at his own mother, Lane would have traded his.

He had once suggested trading Stan Musial, before being blocked by St. Louis Cardinals owner Gussie Busch. Lane, who made over 400 trades in more than 40 years of major league front office work, was the Cleveland general manager when he sent manager Joe Gordon to Detroit for Tigers skipper Jimmie Dykes in August of 1960.

Four months earlier, Lane had made what was likely his most unpopular deal, swapping 1959 American League home run king Rocky Colavito to Detroit for 1959 AL batting champ Harvey Kuenn. Colavito was a tremendous fan favorite in Cleveland, and the Indians' faithful never forgave Lane.

Bill DeWitt gets a giant-sized "What Was He Thinking?" trophy for unloading Frank Robinson. The hard-hitting, hard-playing outfielder was only 30 years old at the time of the deal, but DeWitt called him "an old 30."

The Cincinnati general manager sent Robinson to Baltimore for pitchers Milt Pappas and Jack Baldschun and outfielder Dick Simpson in December of 1965.

Robinson, coming off a season in which he batted .296 with 33 home runs and 113 RBIs for the Reds, won the Triple Crown in his first year with the Orioles, while leading his team to a World Series Championship. Robinson's season was truly one of the greatest of all time. He belted 49 home runs, 10 more than the AL runner up, Harmon Killebrew, and 15 more than the third-place finisher, teammate Boog Powell.

Pappas went 30-29 in two and a half seasons with Cincinnati, Baldschun was 1-5 for the Reds in barely more than a season, and Simpson batted .246 with five homers and 20 RBIs in two years with Cincinnati.

Although there is no question that DeWitt's trade of Robinson was the dumbest of the decade, the most remembered 1960s deal may be the one that sent speedy outfielder Lou Brock from the Chicago Cubs to the St. Louis Cardinals. The transaction sparked the Cardinals to the National League pennant and a World Series championship, and was Brock's springboard to Cooperstown.

Usually referenced as Brock for pitcher Ernie Broglio, the trade also included four other players, with St. Louis packaging Broglio with

39-year-old left-handed pitcher Bobby Shantz and outfielder Doug Clemens and the Cubs sending pitchers Paul Toth and Jack Spring along with Brock. The contributions of those four players to their new clubs were totally forgettable.

On the surface, the deal made sense from Chicago's standpoint. The Cubs had grown impatient with Brock, feeling he struck out too much and was not developing as fast as they had expected.

Broglio, a right-hander, was off to a slow start in 1964, but he was an 18-game winner the previous year and had won 21 games in 1960. Cubs general manager John Holland and Cards GM Bing Devine made the swap on June 15, 1964.

In addition to being an all-time great base stealer and World Series performer, Lou Brock covered a lot of ground in the St. Louis Cardinals' outfield. (National Baseball Hall of Fame and Museum)

Brock was hitting .251 at the time with two home runs. The change of scenery obviously helped. He went bonkers with the Cardinals, batting .348 in 103 games, with 12 homers, 33 stolen bases, and 81 runs scored.

Inserted into the second spot in the lineup behind Curt Flood, Brock became a catalyst for the Cards' offense in their drive to the 1964 pennant and ultimately was inducted into the Hall of Fame, after accumulating more than 3000 hits and 900 stolen bases in his career.

Milt Pappas won 209 games and racked up 43 shutouts in his career. (National Baseball Hall of Fame and Museum)

While there was no complaint with Ken Boyer winning the '64 MVP Award in the National League, it did seem strange that Brock placed tenth in the voting, despite putting together perhaps the most impactful stretch of anyone in baseball that season.

When Brock was traded from the Cubs to the Cardinals on June 15, 1964, St. Louis was 28-31 and seven games out of first place.

From that point, the Cards played .631 baseball (65-38) and shot up all the way to first place in the standings. And Lou Brock was the driving force. His stats and his presence were dazzling. It's hard to imagine St. Louis winning the pennant without Brock. And hard to believe that nine National League players did more for their teams that year.

Broglio won just seven games in two and a half seasons for the Cubs before retiring from baseball. Strangely enough, Devine, who was later called "a mastermind" for pulling off the trade, was fired by St. Louis owner Gussie Busch two months after the deal was made.

The third megatrade of the decade saw the Cardinals once again getting a shining star while losing little. And once again, St. Louis added a hugely productive offensive cog in return for a pitcher who was on the fritz.

Ray Sadecki for Orlando Cepeda, straight up. St. Louis GM Bob Howsam and his San Francisco counterpart, Chub Feeney, made the deal four weeks into the 1966 season. Cepeda was 28 years old, Sadecki was 25. The lefty had been a 20-game winner for the Cardinals two years earlier before falling to 5-8 in 1965. Cepeda had slugged 222 home runs, while averaging more than 100 RBIs and over .300 his first seven years with the Giants.

A knee injury, which ultimately required surgery, ruined Cepeda's '65 season. The Giants had Willie McCovey to play first base, which was Cepeda's best position. The club always seemed to have power-hitting outfielders waiting in the wings.

But the real reason Feeney moved the Baby Bull may have been his discontentment. Cepeda's clubhouse demeanor changed after San Francisco manager Al Dark made an insulting remark about African Americans and Latin Americans in 1964. Cepeda did not get over that and was not a happy Giant from that point on.

In his second full season with the Cardinals, they won the 1967 World Series, Cepeda's MVP performance one of the major reasons they got there. Sadecki was seven games under .500 in three-plus years with the Giants.

Cepeda was traded again before the decade ended. St. Louis sent him to Atlanta for Joe Torre before the 1969 season, and Cepeda was a major factor in the Braves winning the National League East Division title that year.

With the 1960 season under way, the Chicago Cubs made an unusual swap with themselves . . . within their organization, anyway. The Cubs took Lou Boudreau from behind the WGN radio microphone to become the club's manager.

Boudreau had 15 years of managerial experience and was the player-manager for the 1948 Cleveland Indians when they won the World Series. He traded placed with Cubs manager Charlie Grimm, who left the dugout for the broadcast booth.

A trade that was not made loomed mighty large, in the fate of the two players involved and of the two principal teams, as the early part of the decade unfolded.

The Trade That Wasn't also helped write one of the most important sagas in baseball history.

The proposed deal almost took place on December 10, 1959, when Pittsburgh general manager Joe L. Brown was ready to send shortstop Dick Groat to the Kansas City Athletics for outfielder Roger Maris. But Pirates manager Danny Murtaugh talked Brown out of it.

"The way I understand it," Groat would recall, "it was actually a done deal. Joe Brown and Danny Murtaugh were in the hotel room of the Kansas City guys. They agreed to make the trade. The Kansas City guys asked if Joe and Danny would step outside for just a few minutes while they discussed something.

"Joe and Danny went out in the hall and shut the door, and Danny told Joe not to do it. 'I don't want to make this trade,' Danny said. So they go back in the room, and Joe said, 'The deal is off.' And that was that."

The next day, the Athletics traded Maris to the New York Yankees along with infielder Joe DeMaestri and first baseman Kent Hadley for Don Larsen, who would pitch the only perfect game in World Series history, first baseman Marv Throneberry, and outfielders Hank Bauer and Norm Siebern.

Groat and Maris went on to earn Most Valuable Player Awards in 1960. Maris, who had hit 16 home runs and driven in 72 for Kansas City in 1959, clouted 39 homers and had 112 RBIs in his first year with the Yankees.

Maris' second season in pinstripes would make even bigger headlines as the shy outfielder tried to fend off the hungry press while engaged in two home run duels: one with the ghost of The Babe and the other with teammate Mickey Mantle.

Groat led the National League with a .325 batting average in 1960 and anchored Pittsburgh's infield.

The Pirates did trade him two years later, sending the shortstop to St. Louis along with reliever Diomedes Olivo for right-handed pitcher Don Cardwell and shortstop Julio Gotay.

Bad deal for the Buccos, though Cardwell did win 33 games in his four seasons as a Pirate, but Gotay did nothing. Groat was an instant smash in St. Louis.

But he was packing again after three years as a Cardinal, heading for Philadelphia in the fall of 1965 along with Bill White for three players.

White was three months short of his 32nd birthday and coming off four fine years with the Cardinals. The Gold Glove first baseman drove in over 100 runs in Philly before his career declined appreciably.

The Minnesota Twins pulled off a big deal in the middle of the 1964 season when they acquired Jim Grant from Cleveland. The pitcher known as Mudcat had won 64 games in years as a member of the Indians' rotation, but was getting hit hard pretty regularly.

About to turn 29, Grant turned it around with the Twins. He won 11 games and had a sub-.300 ERA the rest of the season, then pitched splendidly in 1965.

The right-hander went 21-7 and threw six shutouts in 270 innings, helping Minnesota to the World Series. He pitched two complete-game victories and hit a three-run homer in the Series, one the Dodgers won in seven games.

The Twins got rid of Grant after the 1967 season, swapping him to the Dodgers. They made him available in the 1968 expansion draft, and Montreal took Grant with the 36th pick. He was dealt one more time in the decade, becoming a Cardinal during the '69 season.

Talk about a steal. How about the trade Baltimore's Harry Dalton made in December of 1968. The Orioles' general manager sent outfielder Curt Blefary and a minor leaguer to Houston for two minor league players and Mike Cuellar.

Cuellar, a 31-year-old left-hander, had won 37 games in four years with the Astros, 16 of them in 1967. After he fell to 8-11 the next season, they let him go.

Cuellar won 23 games along with the American League Cy Young Award his first year as an Oriole. He won 67 over his first three seasons with Baltimore and chalked up 125 victories in six years, an average of nearly 21 per season!

A big name who wasn't big at the time was the key player in a 1966 deal. **Ferguson Jenkins**, a right-handed pitcher, had won six games in parts of three seasons with Philadelphia.

In April, the Phillies swapped him to the Cubs, along with two other players, for pitchers Larry Jackson and Bob Buhl. Jenkins won six that season before winning 20 or more six consecutive years.

His 24–13 with a 2.77 ERA earned him a Cy Young Award in 1971, and his career totals of 284 wins and 4,500 innings pitched helped land him in the Hall of Fame. Jenkins was known for his pinpoint control, and he totaled more than 3,000 strikeouts in his career while walking fewer than 1,000.

Chapter 4

1961: Roger, Vada, and "Diamond Jim"

Roger Maris, a shy guy who never liked being noticed, is known for rewriting a page of the record book, and after he did it, there was much discussion about how that page would look.

Major League Baseball Commissioner Ford Frick did not want the New York Yankees' right fielder to break Babe Ruth's single-season record of 60 home runs set in 1927.

Maris and teammate Mickey Mantle were both on a torrid home run pace in 1961, and Maris ended up hitting 61, Mantle 54. Frick, who had once been a ghost writer for Ruth, said in July of that season that any player hitting more than 60 home runs in 154 games would be cited as holding the new record. (Teams had played 154 games in a season until 1961 expansion increased schedules to 162 games.)

The Commissioner added that if a player hit the 60 mark after his team had played 154 games, there would have to be some distinctive mark in the record books.

Following Frick's announcement, New York sportswriter Dick Young suggested an asterisk be used as the "distinctive mark," but that did not happen. Record books simply used footnotes to denote the extra games. There was never an infamous asterisk placed by Maris' name. It is only mythical.

MARIS SMACKED ANOTHER HOME RUN in the 1961 World Series as the New York Yankees methodically did away with the Cincinnati Reds in five games. Hector Lopez and Johnny Blanchard enjoyed big days with the bat, while Whitey Ford did what he normally did in October.

Coming off a 25–4 record, the crafty left-hander pitched 14 shutout innings in the Series, winning twice and breaking Babe Ruth's record for consecutive scoreless World Series innings.

VADA PINSON WAS ONE OF the keys to the Reds reaching the World Series that year, and he was also one of many interesting stories that unfolded in the 1960s. He lost star status almost overnight during the decade, at the tender age of 27, just when he was expected to be reaching his prime.

Pinson's career started fast. In his first full season in 1959, he led all major league players in runs scored, doubles, and at-bats, while placing in the top five in hits, triples, extra-base hits, and total bases.

Pinson's 96 at-bats as a 19-year-old the previous season made him ineligible for the Rookie of the Year Award, which he certainly would have won otherwise. Instead it went to none other than future Hall of Famer **Willie McCovey**. McCovey was a late call up and played in only 52 games, though he did smack 13 home runs and drive in 38 runs in just 192 at-bats, while batting a sizzling .354.

Pinson played 154 games, hitting .316 with 205 hits, 131 runs scored, 47 doubles, 20 homers, and 84 RBIs in 648 at-bats.

Two years later he batted .343, finishing second in the batting race and third in the MVP voting (behind teammate Frank Robinson and runner-up **Orlando Cepeda**) as the Reds won the National League pennant.

In Pinson's first five full seasons in Cincinnati, he amassed 985 base hits, more than Stan Musial, Willie Mays, Hank Aaron, and Frank Robinson during that period.

Pinson is one of only two players in National League history to finish his career with at least 2,700 hits, 250 home runs, 450 doubles, 100 triples, and 300 steals. The other is Willie Mays.

Pinson compiled a stat sheet from 1959–65 that was better than Mantle's and every other big league center fielder, with the exception of Mays. During that seven-year stretch, Pinson averaged 194 hits, 105 runs, 27 homers, 88 RBIs, and 23 stolen bases. And he was durable, playing an average of 156 games.

Compared to Mantle and Mays because of his blazing speed and home run pop, the left-handed Pinson was beautiful to watch. He glided into the gaps to run down fly balls and was a graceful blur racing from first to third.

Pinson drew criticism because he didn't reprint crackerjack stats every year. Some cited his inconsistency and stubbornness. Over that seven-year span, he had more than 200 hits and batted over .300 in alternate seasons, with off years sandwiched between.

He was criticized for seldom laying the ball down, saying he did not like to bunt. Not doing so probably took away a substantial number of additional base hits and batting average points.

Pinson's last great season was 1965, when he hit .305 with 204 hits, 22 home runs, and 21 stolen bases.

His 18-year major league career did not end until after the 1975 season, but .288 was the highest he batted over his last 10 years. After hitting 20 or more

Vada Pinson had a Hall-of-Fame start to his career, with 131 runs scored in his first full season, but he plateaued early, and never garnered as much as 20% in HOF voting.

homers six times in seven seasons, he did it just once after 1965.

There were a few things that contributed, at least partially, to Pinson's decline. One was that he never got over having his roommate and close friend, Frank Robinson, traded away.

Another was that Pinson suffered nagging hamstring injuries. And, then, there was the humiliation resulting from a 1962 fight with Cincinnati sports writer Earl Lawson.

Pinson took a swing at Lawson, who swore out a warrant for his arrest (and later dropped the charges). Pinson beat himself up over the incident, calling it the most embarrassing thing in his life.

The Reds swapped Pinson to St. Louis, and after one year with the Cardinals, he spent his last six seasons in the American League.

Although Pinson's lifetime numbers are eye-opening, some are left wondering what might have been. Still, it is worth footnoting how he stacks up with center fielders who are in the Hall of Fame.

There are 18 of them, led in the power department by Willie Mays' 660 home runs, in speed with Max Carey's 738 stolen bases, and in batting average and runs scored with Ty Cobb's .366 and 2,246, respectively.

Pinson's .286 batting average ranks ahead of only three HOF center fielders, but his 256 homers are more than 13 of them hit; his RBI total of 1,169 more than 10 of them produced; his 1,365 runs more than eight of them scored; and his 305 stolen bases more than 11 of them swiped.

THREE DYNAMIC DUOS PROVIDED THE DRIVING force behind the Cincinnati Reds winning the 1961 National League pennant. And, for good measure, manager **Fred Hutchinson** had a secret weapon.

His name was Jerry Lynch, and he was what one might call "an occasional hitter."

Most noticed among the Reds' productive pairs were outfielders Robinson and Pinson, who combined to score 218 runs. Robinson, who hit 37 home runs and drove in 124, was the league's MVP. Pinson, who hit .343 and finished second behind Roberto Clemente (.351) in the batting race, placed third in the voting.

Joey Jay and **Jim O'Toole** formed a nice righty-lefty pitching tandem, winning 40 games between them and throwing a total of 499 innings. Right-hander **Jim Brosnan** and southpaw **Bill Henry** earned 16 saves apiece in a day when there was no gimme for protecting a three-run lead.

Then there was Lynch, a fairly nondescript outfielder with a formidable left-handed bat and a label as a part-timer. Originally property of the New York Yankees, he was picked twice in the Rule 5 draft, first by Pittsburgh in 1953 and then by Cincinnati in '56.

He got over 400 plate appearances with the Reds in 1958 and '59, totaling 33 home runs, then saw his at-bats reduced drastically in 1960.

Lynch began the 1961 season as a specialist. A nice way of saying he was to be used exclusively as a pinch-hitter and only against right-handed pitchers.

The truth was that he was considered more of a secret than a weapon. That changed when Lynch slugged three pinch home runs in the season's first month.

All of his at-bats in Cincinnati's first 41 games came off the bench. However, as he continued to come through with big hits and RBIs, Hutchinson used him more and more.

By the time the last two months of the season rolled around, Lynch was splitting time in left field with right-hand hitting **Wally Post**, who hit 20 home runs that season.

The fact that both enjoyed productive 1961 seasons leads to the assumption that they should be latched together as a fourth productive pair. Which is true, except that wasn't really the case until Lynch started 18 of 23 games in a month-long stretch from the end of August through the end of September. Before that, **Gus Bell** was the left-handed batter in Hutchinson's third-outfielder platoon.

During the crucial late-season month that saw Lynch in the lineup almost every day, the Reds lengthened their National League lead over the second-place Los Angeles Dodgers from one and a half to four and a half games.

Lynch keyed the surge by batting .338 with three home runs, three doubles, and a triple, driving in 11 runs.

The Reds and Giants were 3–3 in their game of September 26 when Lynch belted a two-run homer in the eighth inning. That put Cincinnati in front for good on the way to a 6–3 win which clinched the National League pennant.

For the season, he batted .315 with 13 home runs and 50 RBIs in 210 plate appearances, with those stats further enhanced by lofty on-base and slugging percentages of .407 and .624, respectively.

Lynch's numbers in the pinch were stunning: 404/.525/.851 with five home runs, four doubles, a triple and 25 RBIs, the latter a major league record he shares with **Joe Cronin** and **Rusty Staub**.

Lynch had just 57 hits for the 1961 season, but so many of them played such a large part in Reds victories that he finished 22nd in the MVP voting. Pretty good for a guy who had 181 at-bats.

The World Series did not go well for either Lynch or the Reds. The Yankees beat them in five games, and Lynch had just one walk to show for four pinch-hitting appearances.

Lynch, who died in 2012 at the age of 81, is considered one of the all-time best pinch-hitters with 116 hits, 18 home runs, and 64 runs batted in.

NOBODY MATCHED THE CUBS for wackiness. And nothing wackier than 1961, when for some strange reason, team owner Phil Wrigley ditched the traditional system of running a club from the dugout.

He did away with the manager and replaced him with what he called the College of Coaches. What that amounted to was revolving coaches who took turns being in charge.

Four men did that in '61. Elvin Tappe served the longest term as "head coach," leading the Cubbies to a 42–54 record; Verdie Himsl was 10–21; Harry Craft, 7–9; and Lou Klein, 5–6.

Chicago (64–90) improved four wins over the 1960 club, which was managed by Boudreau and Grimm (the last 17 games). The result was the same in the National League standings, however, seventh place.

The Cubs tried the College of Coaches again in 1962 and flunked again. Tappe (4–16), Klein (12–18), and Charlie Metro (43–69) guided (?) Chicago to a 59–103 record and a ninth-place finish, ahead of only the first-year Mets.

The 1962 Cubs did earn a notable footnote in baseball history, however, as one of their coaches was former Negro Leagues star Buck O'Neil, who that year became the first African American coach in major league history.

Wrigley returned to the norm in 1963, with Bob Kennedy managing the Cubs to an 82–80 season—seventh place, 17 games behind NL champ Los Angeles and only four games out of the first division.

"DIAMOND JIM" GENTILE COULD NOT HAVE PICKED a worse season to have his best year.

The Baltimore Orioles had moved into the high-rent district of the American League at the turn of the decade, finishing in second place in 1960 and third in '61.

It was the first time the franchise had been in the first division since the St. Louis Browns finished third in 1945 and was obviously the best showing for the Orioles, whose initial season in Baltimore was 1954.

A young, talented pitching rotation was the main reason for the rise. Kids named Pappas (Milt) and **Estrada (Chuck)**, and Barber (Steve) and Fisher (Jack) gave the Orioles four aces who didn't have much more experience pitching than they did shaving.

Not coincidentally, a big, raw-boned first baseman had his coming-out party at the same time and became Baltimore's anchor on offense. Gentile gave the Birds some heft by hitting 21 home runs and driving in 98 in 1960.

That was his first year as a regular after serving as **Gil Hodges'** occasional caddy at first base with the Brooklyn Dodgers for a couple of summers.

The Dodgers signed Gentile out of high school in 1952 as a hard-throwing left-handed pitcher. The six-four 215-pounder also swung hard, so hard that he sometimes bruised his hip with the bat when he swung and missed.

Switching to first base, the left-handed batter was a prolific home run hitter in the minor leagues and finally earned himself a promotion to Brooklyn. Mostly, he was a spectator with the Dodgers, except for a trip they took to Japan.

Gentile led the club in homers, RBIs, and batting average during the tour, prompting Brooklyn teammate Roy Campanella to dub the first baseman "Diamond" because the catcher felt he was a diamond in the rough.

But after two seasons with very little action and one homer in the majors, the Dodgers traded Gentile to Baltimore.

He followed his big rookie season with an even bigger 1961 performance, ending with numbers that normally would have garnered Most Valuable Player and Player of the Year trophies.

But, of course, a couple of guys named Maris and Mantle relegated Diamond Jim to the background.

In a season that saw him become the first major leaguer ever to hit two grand slams in the same game (in successive at-bats), Gentile just kept slugging. He ended 1961 with 46 homers, 141 RBIs, a .302 batting average, and five grand slams. Along the way, he made the American League All-Star team. He finished third in the MVP voting behind Maris, who won the award for a second straight year, and Mantle.

In an unusual footnote, in 2010 it was found that Maris was erroneously given an RBI in a July 5, 1961 game in Cleveland. When it was subtracted, Maris had 141 runs batted in for the '61 season, making Gentile the co-league leader in RBIs.

Gentile's contract with the Orioles in 1961 stipulated that he would be paid a $5,000 bonus if he led the league in RBIs. Baltimore presented him with a check for that amount at a 2010 game.

AND THEN THERE WAS **Norm Cash**. Stormin' Norman, as Detroit Tigers broadcasting legend Ernie Harwell nicknamed him. Cash finished fourth in the 1961 American League MVP voting. Like Gentile, he put up numbers that season that would have won the award going away many other years.

The Tigers' first baseman led the AL with a .361 batting average, 193 hits, and .487 on-base percentage. He slammed 41 home runs, drove in 132 runs, and slugged .662.

Cash, whose major league career spanned 17 seasons, would never again hit 40 homers, total 100 RBIs, or bat .300, though he averaged 25 home runs over a 12-year period.

STARTING IN 1961—**Billy Williams, Matty Alou, Joe Torre, Ron Perranoski, Dick Howser**, two **Ken Hunts, Al McBean, Mack Jones, Rollie Sheldon**, Carl Yastrzemski.

Rookies of the Year were Williams and **Don Schwall**, a 6-foot-6 right-hander who won 15 games for the Boston Red Sox in 1961 and never had another winning season.

Williams, on the other hand—he of the Sweet Swing—was the picture of consistency over a Hall of Fame career that lasted 18 years. One of the all-time Cubs favorites, He hit 20 or more home runs in his first 13 full seasons in the majors, finishing with 426 and a .290 batting average.

Torre also has a Cooperstown plaque—as a manager. His on-the-field numbers were first-rate as well, including an 18-year batting average of .297 with 252 home runs. As the MVP in 1971, he led the National league with 230 hits, 137 RBIs, and a .363 batting average.

Howser batted a career-high .280 as the Kansas City Athletics' regular shortstop, finishing second in the AL Rookie of the Year balloting. He hit .248 in eight seasons as an infielder, then managed the Yankees and Royals to first-place finishes, winning the 1985 World Series with Kansas City.

Ken L. Hunt was a 24-year-old outfielder who hit 25 home runs and drove in 84 runs for the Los Angeles Angels. He hit just eight more homers in parts of three seasons and was out of baseball by the time he was 30.

Ken R. Hunt was a 22-year-old right-handed pitcher who was in the starting rotation most of the season for the National League champion Cincinnati Reds. He got off to a fast start before ending 9–10 with a 3.96 to win The Sporting News Rookie Pitcher of the Year award. Hunt never pitched in the majors after that 1961 season.

ENDING IN 1961—Hank Bauer, **Jim Rivera**, Willie "Puddin' Head" Jones, Ted Kluszewski, **Jackie Jensen, Mike Garcia, Billy Martin, Faye Throneberry, Johnny Antonelli, Walt Dropo, Rip Repulski.**

This may have been Big Klu's first jersey for the Chicago White Sox (1959–1960) as they had some trouble with the spelling of his name. (National Baseball Hall of Fame and Museum)

Kluszewski and Dropo were muscleman first basemen who posted some glossy stats but only for short terms.

Dropo's time on center stage was far more brief. He earned Rookie of the Year honors in 1950 when he popped 34 home runs, drove in an American League-leading 144 runs, and batted .322 for the Red Sox. He never topped .300, 30 homers, or 100 RBIs again.

Big Klu, with the big biceps, slammed 40, 49, and 47 home runs for Cincinnati from 1953–55 and added 35 in '56. He knocked in more than 100 runs all four years, with a high of 141 in 1954.

Kluszewski injured his back in 1956 and never recovered his power, managing a season high of five homers until he hit 15 for the expansion Angels of 1961, his last year in baseball. An extremely good fielding first baseman, Klu batted over .300 seven times and hit .298 for his 15-year career.

Throneberry is worth mentioning mainly because he was the older brother of Mets folk hero Marv Throneberry. Faye was a part-time outfielder who batted .236 over eight years with the Senators, Red Sox, and Angels.

Jensen hated flying. So much that he retired at the age of 32 after averaging 26 home runs and 111 RBIs over six years with the Red Sox. The 1958 American League MVP quit in '59, came back a year later, then quit for good following the '61 season.

Puddin' Head Jones is one of the all-time most colorful baseball nicknames. (He got it as a child from a 1930s song titled "Wooden Head, Puddin' Head Jones".)

He hit 28 home runs for the Phillies' 1950 Whiz Kids and was a reliable defensive third baseman for 10 years in Philadelphia. He had 190 homers in 15 big league seasons.

"Jungle Jim" was another nickname that ranks way up there. It belonged to Rivera, a hard-nosed outfielder who was a double-figure home run hitter five straight years for the Chicago White Sox. He had 16 triples in 1953.

Bauer, the old Marine, played in the shadow of big-name stars with the Yankees. But the right fielder and frequent leadoff man was one of the team's best clutch performers and played on seven World Series champions.

Bauer, who hit four of his seven Series home runs in 1958, managed a World Series champion five years after retiring as a player.

LAST PITCH OF 1961 SEASON—Yankees **Bud Daley** to Reds center fielder Vada Pinson. Pinson flied out to **Hector Lopez** in short left field. Daley, a left-hander, pitched six and two-thirds innings of relief in Game Five as the World Series concluded at Cincinnati's Crosley Field. New York won, 13–5.

Chapter 5

Expanding Horizons

New York City has long been considered the hub of big league baseball. The obvious reason is the tremendous attraction of the Yankees, who are somewhat of an international synonym for baseball because of their dynastic success and because they have had iconic players like **Babe Ruth**, Mickey Mantle, and **Derek Jeter**.

New York also was the place where the most big league baseball was played for 55 years.

Beginning in 1903, New York was the home of three major league teams. Brooklyn (with nicknames like the Bridegrooms, Superbas, Trolley Dodgers, and Robins before adopting the Dodgers) and the New York Giants had both been in the National League since 1890.

The American League, which began play in 1901, has had a New York franchise more than a century. The Baltimore Orioles moved to New York in 1903 and became the Highlanders. They changed their nickname to the Yankees in 1913.

The Yankees, Dodgers, and Giants stayed together in New York until the two National League clubs moved to the West Coast following the 1957 season.

The Giants and Dodgers formed an instant and bitter rivalry as they battled for National League pennants. The Dodgers would then forge a dogged fall rivalry with the Yankees, those two teams meeting in five World Series before Brooklyn won one.

The Yankees and Giants squared off in six Fall Classics while both resided in New York, the Giants winning the first two and the Yankees the last four.

The Dodgers finally beat the Yankees in a World Series, but amazingly, Brooklyn's home attendance for the 1955 championship season was its lowest in eight years.

Dodgers majority owner Walter O'Malley wanted to relocate in Brooklyn and even obtained a model for a domed stadium to be built there. He found a suitable site at the corner of Flatbush and Atlantic Avenues.

As it turned out, finding a suitable piece of real estate was the least of O'Malley's problems. He needed the help of a powerful man named Robert Moses to obtain the land. It was too expensive for O'Malley, who hoped Moses would condemn the property, thereby lowering the price.

Moses, whose numerous titles included Commissioner of New York City Parks, was not particularly interested in sports. He wanted to use the Flatbush property, where the 1939–40 World's Fair was held, for a parking garage and felt any new stadium should be built in Flushing Meadows.

O'Malley, who understood that the Dodgers could not go to Los Angeles unless another major league team also moved to California, encouraged Stoneham to relocate in San Francisco. Stoneham accommodated, taking his Giants to join the Dodgers on the West Coast for the 1958 season.

The departures of the Giants and Dodgers left New York with just one big league team and without its long-standing National League rivalry.

Major league baseball's first modern-day expansion did not just happen overnight. It was not simply the result of a shrewd job of blackmailing by William Shea and renowned baseball man Branch Rickey.

They did not hold Commissioner Ford Frick and 16 team owners hostage by threatening to start a new league. The shadow of the prospective Continental League was not so ominous that major league officials threw up their hands and said, "Okay, let's have four new teams."

However, the threat of a new league certainly put baseball's pedal to the expansion's metal.

There had been talk of expansion for some time, especially after the Dodgers moved from Brooklyn to Los Angeles and the Giants from New York City to San Francisco.

Lawyer William Shea, who was appointed New York City Baseball Commissioner by Mayor Robert Wagner, tried hard to bring a National League team to his city.

He attempted to lure the Philadelphia Phillies, Cincinnati Reds, and Pittsburgh Pirates to New York. He talked to National League executives about expanding.

In November of 1958, Shea proposed the idea of a third major league, and in July of 1959, there was an official announcement of the organization of the Continental League.

Then, in August, Branch Rickey, called the Mahatma because of his deep Christian faith and numerous achievements, was introduced as the league's president. Shea needed some clout and credibility, and who would have more of both than Rickey?

Even at the age of 77, he was a formidable presence. He was a proven baseball man, shrewd, innovative, and bold. He had made a substantial impact on baseball, first by conceiving and building the game's first farm system and then by breaking baseball's color barrier.

Rickey and Shea met with United States Senator Estes Kefauver and House of Representatives member Emmanuel Cellar, both of whom were on the Subcommittee for the Study of Monopoly Power, which had held hearings involving Major League Baseball in the early 1950s.

Rickey asked major league owners for their cooperation in starting the Continental League. On the surface, Major League Baseball officials agreed, but in reality, they were not about to do anything that would undermine their own interests.

The owners were very upset, realizing they could lose money and players. Owners were concerned that some of their players might be lured away by the new league and that many others would have to be paid higher salaries to stay with their major league teams.

Major League Baseball wanted the Continental League teams taking up residence in cities where there were already minor league teams to pay stiff fees for territorial rights.

New York was to be one of the Continental League members, joining Dallas, Denver, Atlanta, Houston, Minneapolis-St. Paul, Buffalo, and Toronto. Team owners would each pay $50,000 to the league, with capital investment commitments of $2.5 million apiece.

The major problem for the Continental League was finding players. Its teams might outbid big league clubs for some players, but the majority would have to come from elsewhere.

The minor leagues were an obvious avenue, but players from the minors were under contract to the major league teams because of Major League Baseball's exemption to the reserve clause.

Rickey attempted to organize a minor league for the purpose of developing players in advance of the Continental League opening. Major League Baseball Commissioner Ford Frick stomped down that idea, and Rickey then threatened to raid major league teams for players.

The idea of placing an American League team on the West Coast was particularly appealing. Frick knew Major League baseball's 16 owners could not resist growth forever, and the owners knew it, too.

They were aware that there were millions of fans west of the Mississippi River who were dying to plop into seats at big league stadiums to absorb some of the national pastime atmosphere in person.

The American League had an eye on Minneapolis-St. Paul for quite a while and came up with the idea of adding one new team in each league. Minneapolis would join the AL, with New York becoming the ninth National League franchise.

National League President Warren Giles at first opposed the idea of expansion, saying his league had no reason to consider it. But it was not long before he was telling the prospective third league to put up or shut up, and that if the former did not happen soon, the National League was ready to adopt two of the cities high on the list of Continental planners.

There is no doubt that expansion would have taken place eventually. Shea, who was designated as New York City's recruiter of a National League team, had tried everything he could think of to get a National League franchise back in his city.

Finally, the thinking was that if there was no major league in which New York could play, a new major league could be built for New York. Shea and Rickey accelerated the expansion process by peddling the Continental League.

Major league owners were not ready to add new teams, but they did not like the alternative of having eight new cities with which to share the wealth, rather than four.

And so it was that big league baseball changed forever on July 18, 1960. That was when the National League, at its meeting in Chicago, voted to expand from eight to 10 teams by 1962.

At that meeting, Giles challenged the Continental League by saying if it was not prepared to operate in the near future, the National League was ready to expand. All eight National League owners voted to do so.

The National League voted to add two new teams, and the American League then did the same. Major League Baseball promised the Continental League that expansion would add four new big league teams.

That, indeed, became a reality by 1962, when the New York Mets and Houston Colt 45's joined the National League, following the 1961 addition of the Los Angeles Angels and Washington Senators to the American League.

The Continental League officially disbanded in August of 1960, never having played a game, but its original mission had been accomplished. A National League team would return to New York City. Also, major league expansion took place faster than it would have without the threat of a third league.

The American League then held closed-door meetings on October 10, 1960, to consider proposals from Minneapolis-St. Paul, Dallas-Fort Worth, and Houston.

The following day, New York and Houston petitioned the National League for franchises. On October 27, the American League awarded franchises to Los Angeles and Washington, D.C., the latter replacing the old Senators, who would move from the nation's capital to Minneapolis (to be called the Twins).

New York officially returned to the National League on March 6, 1961. Giles announced that the Metropolitan Baseball Club, Inc., was an official league member, with privileges including a franchise to operate a professional baseball club in the City of New York.

The team would be known as the Mets. There was historical significance to the nickname as the New York Metropolitans had played in the American Association from 1880–87.

Mrs. Joan Whitney Payson was the Mets' owner. She was a rich heiress who had owned 10 percent of the New York Giants baseball team and sold it in order to buy 85 percent of the prospective New York entry into the Continental League. When the Continental League folded, Mrs. Payson had herself a major league baseball team.

The new Washington Senators' owner was Bob Short. Calvin Griffith owned the Senators-turned-Twins. On December 6, the Los Angeles franchise, to be called the Angels, went to cowboy crooner and movie star Gene Autry.

The American League would begin play in the 1961 season with 10 teams. The National League would do the same the following year. Putting together two teams in such a short time was a rush job for the American League. The season was months away, and the brand-new franchises did not even have one single player.

The original plan was for the league's expansion teams to begin play in 1962, along with the National League's two new teams. But part of a deal that allowed the Senators to move to Minnesota and become the Twins for the 1961 season provided the expansion Senators to begin the same year so Washington would not be without a major league team.

Griffith Stadium continued to be the home of the Senators, just a different version. The Angels had planned on sharing Dodger Stadium with their National League counterpart in 1961, but that ballpark was not ready.

So the Angels played their first season in Wrigley Field, which had been used by the Hollywood Stars of the Pacific Coast League. The Wrigley Field in Los Angeles was a carbon copy (although smaller) of the Cubs' Wrigley Field in Chicago.

On December 14, 1960, an expansion draft was held to stock the Los Angeles Angels and Washington Senators. The eight American League teams were required to pull seven players apiece from active rosters (as of August 31, 1960) and eight additional players from their 40-man rosters and make them available for the draft.

The Senators and Angels would pay $75,000 each for 28 players they took in the draft. No more than seven major league players could be taken from any existing team. Both expansion franchises were required to pick at least 10 pitchers, two catchers, six infielders, and four outfielders.

Los Angeles and Washington also had the option of drafting one non-roster player from each existing team at a price of $25,000.

The Angels made **Eli Grba** the first player ever chosen in a major league expansion draft. A sub-.500 pitcher with control troubles, the 26-year-old right-hander was taken from the New York Yankees. Perhaps the notion that the Yanks saw something in him was the impetus behind the Angels' decision.

Grba was signed by the Boston Red Sox in 1952 and traded to the Yankees in 1957. He pitched 131 innings and compiled an 8–9 record, walking 30 more than he struck out, while appearing in 39 games with the Yanks over the combined 1959 and 1960 seasons.

Players in the draft who had been stars but were past their prime included Ted Kluszewski, **Dale Long**, **Eddie Yost**, Bobby Shantz, **Tom Sturdivant**, and **Bob Cerv**.

Big Klu averaged 43 home runs and 116 RBIs in a four-year stretch with the slugging Cincinnati Reds. Long set a major league record (since equaled by Don Mattingly and Ken Griffey Jr.) by hitting a home run in eight consecutive games for Pittsburgh in 1956.

Shantz was the American League MVP in 1954 when he won 24 games for the Philadelphia Athletics, then managed more than seven victories only once over the last 11 years of his career.

Yost, the third baseman known as the "Walking Man," had drawn an average of 119 bases on balls for Washington and Detroit over an 11-year span. Cerv clouted 38 home runs one year for Kansas City, jokingly called a Yankee "farm team" because of the frequency with which players shuffled back and forth between K.C. And New York. He was on the Yankees three different times.

Sturdivant won 16 games in back-to-back seasons for pennant-winning Yankee teams, but won just eight games over the next three years. He was the kid of this group at age 30. The others were at least 34.

The Angels used their No. 13 pick to get Yost, their No. 18 to get Cerv, and their No. 23 to get Kluszewski. But they really cleaned up on youngsters.

Los Angeles grabbed **Jim Fregosi** from Boston after the Red Sox had signed him a year earlier, right-hander **Dean Chance** from Baltimore after the Orioles had signed him almost two years earlier, and **Buck Rodgers** from Detroit.

Fregosi, who was 19, would be the Angels' regular shortstop for nine years. Chance, who was 20, would be their ace pitcher for five years before being traded to Minnesota. Rodgers, 22, had played five years on Detroit farm teams. He would be the Angels' everyday catcher for six seasons.

The most productive early selection by L.A. was **Ken McBride**, 25, taken with the seventh pick. The right-handed pitcher, who worked 27 innings in parts of two seasons with the Chicago White Sox, averaged a dozen wins over his first three years with the Angels.

They used another pitcher drafted from the White Sox, **Jim McAnany**, to get outfielder **Lou Johnson** in a trade with the Cubs. Then, two days after their first season opened, the Angels swapped Johnson to Toronto of the International League for **Leon Wagner**, a left-handed hitter who had clouted 51 home runs in the Carolina League in 1956.

Wagner had accumulated 448 at-bats in three years in the big leagues, establishing himself as an all-hit, no-field outfielder by totaling 22 home runs and 10 errors. He hit 28 homers and drove in 79 runs for Los Angeles in 1961, with six errors.

Ken Hunt, a promising outfielder, had two brief stays with the Yankees. With L.A., he broke in with a boom, bashing 25 home runs and leading the club with 84 RBIs. His combined stats over the next three years (they were also his last three) did not come close to equaling 1961.

The Angels drafted catcher **Earl Averill Jr.** and first baseman **Steve Bilko**, a couple of journeymen with reputations but without major league success.

Averill was the son of the Hall of Fame outfielder by the same name. Bilko, a 250-pounder, had slugged 148 home runs over a three-year period in the minor leagues, but had managed just 48 in 1,280 big league at-bats.

The Thomas boys were terrific finds for L.A. Not related, Lee and George both joined the club via transactions after the 1961 season was under way.

Lee Thomas, a left-handed hitter with a good bat and bad glove, had languished seven years on Yankee farms. In May, the Angels obtained him, hard-throwing, hard-living reliever **Ryne Duren**, and pitcher

Johnny James from New York for Cerv and another drafted player, pitcher **Tex Clevenger**.

They purchased George Thomas, who played third base and the outfield, from Detroit in late June. The Tigers' bonus baby had one major league at-bat since signing in 1957.

Lee hit 24 home runs, George 13, Averill 21, and Bilko 20. Led by Wagner and Hunt, the Angels hit 189 home runs—second in the American League only to the mighty Yankees—and scored the fourth-most runs in the league.

They also led the American League in strikeouts at the plate and on the mound. The Angels got 12 wins from McBride and 11 each from Grba and **Ted Bowsfield**, a lefty picked up from the Cleveland Indians as part of the expansion draft but after the draft's completion.

Managed by Bill Rigney, the former Giants' infielder and skipper, the Angels enjoyed some immediate success. They won 70 games in their first season, and finished in eighth place in the 10-team American League, 38 and a half games behind the pennant-winning Yankees and nine games ahead of Washington and Kansas City, who shared the cellar.

Los Angeles used 46 players in 1961, including 18 pitchers. McBride and Duren, he of the thick-lensed glasses, represented the Angels on the American League All-Star team.

The club pulled off a shocking 1962, staying in the American League pennant race much of the season before finishing in third place with 86 wins.

Wagner and Lee Thomas combined to slam 63 home runs in '62, driving in more than 100 runs apiece, while rookie Chance won 14 games to lead a pitching staff that posted the second-stingiest earned run average in the league.

Whereas the Angels had five players to hit 20 or more home runs in 1961, the Senators had none. Six Angels had at least 59 RBIs. Two Senators had that many. The Angels had three pitchers with double-figure victory totals. The Senators had none; in fact, no Washington hurler won more than six games.

Washington's first selection in the expansion draft was Shantz, who was traded two days later to Pittsburgh for **Bennie Daniels**, **R.C. Stevens**, and **Harry Bright**.

Daniels would lead Senators pitchers in 1961 with 12 wins. Washington used its No. 14 pick to take Yankees' spare part Dale Long, who hit 17 home runs that season, as did outfielder Willie Tasby, snared from the Red Sox with the No. 19 selection.

He was 28 years old, the same age as No. 23 pick **Gene Green**, who was one of six additional selections taken by the Senators. Green, a catcher by trade, came over from Baltimore and also played some outfield. He led Washington with 18 homers and had 62 RBIs, one less than team leader Tasby.

Dick Donovan, who had enjoyed some success with the White Sox, was not taken until the fourth-from-the-last selection in the draft. He went 10–10 in his only season with the Senators and led the American League with a 2.40 earned run average.

The very next year, Donovan won 20 for Cleveland. Daniels and **Joe McClain**, two other members of the starting rotation, allowed fewer than four earned runs per nine innings and were the main reasons Washington's team ERA was sixth-best in the league.

The new Senators, who were managed by two-time American League batting champion Mickey Vernon, ended their first season tied for last place at 61–100, while the old Senators—the Twins—finished 70–90 and in seventh place. Proving they were no fluke, the Senators lost 101 games in 1962 and had the basement all to themselves.

The New York Mets and the Houston Colt 45s stocked their rosters with players selected in the first National League expansion draft which took place October 10, 1961, at the Netherland-Hilton Hotel in Cincinnati.

Houston won the coin toss and used the first pick to take shortstop **Eddie Bressoud** from San Francisco, trading him five weeks later for Red Sox shortstop **Don Buddin**.

The Colt 45s added more infielders with their next two selections, getting third baseman **Bob Aspromonte** from the Dodgers and **Bob Lillis**, still another shortstop, from the Cardinals.

Roman Mejias, an outfielder destined to be a backup with the Pirates, was Houston's sixth pick. He led the first-year Colt 45s in hitting, runs scored, home runs, RBIs, and stolen bases, but also committed the second-most errors among National League outfielders.

The first three pitchers drafted by the Colt 45s vanished quickly. **Dick Drott**, a right-hander who showed tremendous promise as a Cubs rookie before encountering arm problems, was Houston's fourth pick. He went down with an injury after pitching 13 innings.

Left-hander Shantz, who joined **Gene Woodling** as the only players picked in the initial expansion drafts of both the American and National League, went at No. 11. Shantz threw a complete game on opening day, then was traded to St. Louis in early May.

Roman Mejias's 24 home runs in 1962 tied him for 14th in the NL, but he was out of the majors just two years and 13 home runs later.

In return, the Colt 45s got outfielder **Carl Warwick**, who won a starting outfield job and hit 16 home runs. Righty pitcher **Sad Sam Jones** was grabbed by Houston with its No. 13 selection, and he was traded to Detroit in December for two players.

One of them was **Bob Bruce**, another right-hander, whose 10 wins tied **Turk Farrell** for the most on the 1961 Colt 45s.

Although they finished at or near the bottom of the National League in most of the offensive categories, the Colt 45s were able to finish in eighth place in the standings because of solid pitching.

Led by Farrell, who struck out 203 batters and had a 3.02 earned run average despite losing 20 games, Houston's staff posted a 3.83 ERA and notched the second-most strikeouts in the National League.

Manager **Harry Craft** had a capable bullpen of veterans, led by former Braves closer Don McMahon, and they bailed the starters out of numerous jams.

The club played its first three seasons in Colt Stadium, known for poor lighting, thick clouds of mosquitoes, and unbearably high temperatures and humidity. The park was built for pitchers as it measured 360 feet down each foul line, from 395 to 427 feet in the alleys, and 420 to straightaway center field.

The Mets' brain trust was headed up by general manager George Weiss and manager Casey Stengel, both of whom had been dismissed by the New York Yankees after they lost the 1960 World Series to the Pittsburgh Pirates.

The Mets spent $1.8 million to draft 22 players. They used their first pick to take San Francisco Giants catcher **Hobie Landrith**. Stengel justified the selection of Landrith—a lifetime .237 hitter with 28 home runs in more than 1,600 at-bats—by saying, "You gotta have a catcher or you will have a lot of passed balls."

The New York Mets, sure to bring back visions of the old days by playing their first two seasons in the Polo Grounds, largely traveled down memory lane in piecing together their initial roster.

New York chose speedy **Elio Chacon**, an infielder who had trouble communicating with outfielders on fly balls because he spoke so little English, from Cincinnati in the second round. The biggest name on the Mets' list of used-to-be's was Gil Hodges, the slugging first baseman for so many of the pennant-winning Brooklyn teams.

Others who had enjoyed considerable big league success were outfielders Gus Bell and **Lee Walls**, infielders **Don Zimmer** and **Felix Mantilla**, and pitchers Roger Craig and Jay Hook.

Hodges, who was 38, had hit 361 home runs for the Dodgers, helping them win six National League pennants and the 1955 World Series. Bell had hit 200 homers, most of them for the Cincinnati Reds.

Craig, a right-handed pitcher, had won 49 games for the Dodgers and was with them for three pennants. He was 32 when the 1962 season opened.

The Mets added **Charlie Neal**, Richie Ashburn, and **Frank Thomas** in late 1961 transactions, and they dealt for **Wilmer "Vinegar Bend" Mizell** after their inaugural season began.

Ashburn was the only eventual Hall of Fame member among the original Mets. They purchased the lifetime .308 hitter, who played 12 years with the Philadelphia Phillies, from the Chicago Cubs.

Thomas played third base, first, and the outfield. He had hit 223 home runs in nine years as an everyday player. The Mets obtained him from the Braves for cash and a player to be named later who turned out to be Gus Bell.

Neal had been the Dodgers' regular second baseman four years. He was Brooklyn's shortstop most of 1957, when an aging **Pee Wee Reese** was moved to third base. Neal was acquired by the Mets for Walls and $100,000.

The Mets also bought pitcher **Billy Loes** from the San Francisco Giants for $25,000. A right-hander who was plagued by arm miseries throughout his career, Loes won 10 or more games four straight seasons for the Brooklyn Dodgers and had 80 big league victories in 11 years. Pitching in three World Series for the Dodgers, he had an eight-inning, eight-strikeout performance to beat the Yankees in the 1953 Fall Classic.

Quoted in the newspapers before the 1952 World Series as having picked the Yankees to win in seven games, Loes was confronted by his Brooklyn manager **Charlie Dressen**. Loes told Dressen that he had been misquoted . . . that he had actually picked the Yankees in six games.

He once said that he never wanted to be a 20-game winner because then he would be expected to do it every year. When notified that his contract had been purchased by the Mets, Loes said, "The Mets is a good thing. They give everybody jobs. Just like the WPA (Works Progress Administration)."

In February of 1962, Loes told the Mets that his sore arm would prevent him from pitching, and he retired from baseball. The Giants had to return the $25,000 to New York.

In a transaction that was amusingly symbolic of their first season, the Mets even traded a player for himself, the only time that has happened in major league history. They acquired catcher **Harry Chiti** from the Cleveland Indians in April of 1962 for cash and a player to be named later. That player turned out to be Chiti, who was returned to the Indians two months later.

Marv Throneberry became practically a mascot for the Mets as his frequent blunders typified the team's ineptness, and his initials (his middle name was Eugene) spelled M-E-T.

A first baseman who came up in the Yankees' farm system, he slammed 82 home runs in two seasons for Triple-A Denver. He played part-time for the Yanks for two years and also spent time with Kansas City and Baltimore, hitting 37 homers and striking out one out every four trips to the plate.

In May of 1962, the Orioles traded Throneberry to the Mets for Hobie Landrith and cash. Marvelous Marv, as he adoringly came to be known to Mets fans, played 97 games at first base for New York that season.

He made 17 errors, giving him a .981 fielding percentage that would be the lowest for first basemen in the majors over the next 17 years. On more than one occasion, he smacked an extra-base hit, only to be called out for missing a base.

Once, when he wound up on third with an apparent triple, he was called out for failing to touch second base. When Stengel came out to argue, an umpire told him, "Don't bother, Casey; he missed first, too."

New York signed **Ed Kranepool** for $85,000 in June of 1962 right out of James Monroe High School in the Bronx, where he was born and grew up. He was only 17 and was the same age when he got six at-bats, a double among them, in a September call-up.

Kranepool played his entire 17-year career with the Mets and endured some rocky times along the way as he was sent back to the minors for parts of the 1963 and 1970 seasons.

His best overall season was 1971, when he batted .280 with 14 home runs and 58 RBIs, while leading National League first basemen with a .998 fielding percentage.

Very little attention was paid to the Mets picking up **Rod Kanehl**. In the minor league draft of November 1961, they selected him from the New York Yankees, who had signed him in 1954.

Kanehl was not given much of a chance of making the Mets, but he stuck and ended up playing all four infield positions and all three outfield spots for the new National League team.

A rookie at the age of 28, he was a fan favorite, perhaps the most popular Met in 1962, and a favorite of Stengel as well. Casey loved Kanehl's hustle and feistiness, and he continued to play him in spite of GM George Weiss, who did not feel Kanehl possessed big league talent. But, then, not many other Mets did, either.

The Mets' biggest star was the 71-year-old Stengel, who came out of a one-year retirement to be their manager. He was not hired because of his fabled success with the New York Yankees, and there was no hope that his craftiness could turn a bunch of has-beens into a winning club.

Old Casey was hired to provide entertainment and to keep the Mets in the headlines even if their performance on the field did not. He was a delightful distraction, and he uttered one of his more famous quotes after watching a typical performance by the Mets: "Can't anybody here play this game?" Jimmy Breslin made that line the title of his book on the New York Mets' first season.

Stengel's final record as a manager was 63 games above .500 despite the Mets losing 229 more games than they won while he was with them. They lost at least 109 games in each of his three full seasons as their manager.

Weiss put together a team of over-the-hill guys for the first edition of the Mets. Of course, there was no farm system to develop players, and the other National League clubs certainly were not going to place glittering prospects on the draft market. So, that first year, it was mostly a matter of putting nine men on the field.

There was an obvious Dodgers look to the Mets, whose debut season included appearances by six former Brooklyn players. The hope was that fans would come out to enjoy some nostalgia as they recalled what Hodges, Neal, Craig, **Clem Labine**, Don Zimmer, and **Joe Pignatano** had accomplished at Ebbets Field.

The average age of the eight position players in New York's 1962 opening-day lineup was 32.5. Their future was behind them, evidenced by the fact that those eight players combined to total less than eight full seasons after the 1962 schedule concluded.

The original Mets used 20 players, nine of them pitchers, who never again played in the majors after the '62 season ended. Nine others lasted one more year, with three seeing extremely sparse action in a second additional season.

Of the 45 players used by the Mets in their first year, only 13 were playing appreciable big league roles two years later.

Old Case was as humorous as ever in that first season, and his players were even funnier. The Mets lost their first nine games and won no more than nine in any one month. They placed last in the National League in hitting, pitching, and fielding.

The Mets finished 60 and a half games behind San Francisco, which defeated Los Angeles two games to one in a playoff series to win the pennant.

In the four opening games by the expansion teams in 1961 and '62, Houston and Los Angeles won as Roman Mejias and Ted Kluszewski hit two home runs apiece for the Colt 45s and Angels, respectively.

The Mets gave New York writers something to excite old-days fans as ex-Dodgers Gil Hodges and Charlie Neal hammered home runs.

The Angels were the youngest expansion team, averaging 28.2 years in 1961. The 1962 Mets were next at 29, with the '61 Senators averaging 29.4. The 1962 Colt 45s, at 29.5, were the oldest.

Chapter 6

1962: Keeping Up with Maury

Willie Mays batted .304 in 1962 with 49 home runs, a major league-high 141 RBIs, and 130 runs scored. Tommy Davis knocked in 153 runs that same season, had 230 base hits, batted a major league-high .346, scored 120 runs, and hit 27 home runs. Frank Robinson hit .342, with 208 hits, 134 runs, 39 home runs, and 136 RBIs. Hank Aaron batted .323, scored 127 times, hit 45 home runs, and drove in 128 runs.

None of them won the National League Most Valuable Player Award.

It went to Dodgers shortstop Maury Wills, who stole 104 bases to break **Ty Cobb's** major league record for a season. Wills had 208 hits, 130 runs, and a .299 batting average.

Wills winning the MVP was symbolic of the changing tide of baseball, with the point of emphasis shifting from power to speed.

It should be mentioned, however, that this was one of the most controversial MVP outcomes of all time. Many have argued that Wills did not even have the best season on his own team in 1962.

Tommy Davis' numbers were stupendous. Willie Davis had double figures in doubles, triples, and home runs, while scoring 103 runs, driving in 85, and swiping 32 bases. Don Drysdale won 25 games, pitched 314 innings, and had a 2.83 ERA on the way to a Cy Young Award.

The general feeling is that a substantial number of voters were substantially dazzled by someone stealing more than 100 bases.

One thing not often talked about is what Wills went through on the way to his record. Hank Aaron's travails are well documented regarding his 1974 chase after Babe Ruth's home run record, and Wills experienced similar atrocious threats and insults.

Demeaning and hate-filled letters filled his locker, most from bigots who resented African Americans' success on any level. Many were from the South where the thought of a man of color replacing "one of their own" in the record book was absolute idiocy.

So Wills, in addition to having legs that were beaten, battered, and bruised from all the slides, hard tags, and spike wounds, suffered emotional anguish. All of which took a tremendous toll.

The Dodgers tied San Francisco atop the National League standings, necessitating a best-of-three playoff. Eleven years to the day after Thomson's home run gave the Giants a pennant-deciding win over the Dodgers, the Giants scored four runs in the ninth to take the decisive Game Three and the NL flag.

Two years after serving up the World Series-losing home run to Pittsburgh's Bill Mazeroski, Ralph Terry pitched a four-hitter in Game Seven as the Yankees blanked San Francisco, 1–0. It was Fall Classic championship No. 20 for New York.

The season was highlighted by Mickey Mantle's 400th career home run, the first of Sandy Koufax's four no-hitters, and 40-year-old Warren Spahn's career home run No. 31, setting a National League record for homers by a pitcher.

GENE CONLEY WON 15 games for the 1962 Boston Red Sox, a team that won 76 games and finished eighth in the American League standings. He pitched 241 innings despite experiencing pain in his right arm throughout much of the season. Both figures were career highs.

The 6-foot-8 Conley was a tremendous athlete. In addition to winning 91 games over an 11-year major league career, he played six seasons in the National Basketball Association.

Backing up legend Bill Russell at center and Tommy Heinsohn at power forward, Conley played on three successive Boston Celtics teams that won NBA championships.

Pitching for the 1957 Milwaukee Braves who beat the Yankees in the World Series, he is the only athlete ever to play on championship teams in two professional sports.

A basketball and baseball star at Washington State University, Conley was inducted into the school's hall of fame. In 1951, his first year of pro baseball, he was a 20-game winner and was named the Minor League Player of the Year by The Sporting News.

Gene Conley was on two Boston Celtics championship teams, in addition to winning the World Series with the Milwaukee Braves. (National Baseball Hall of Fame and Museum)

Two years later, the magazine gave the same award to Conley after he won 23 games in the American Association. In 1954, he was in the big leagues to stay, winning 14 games with a 2.96 ERA for the Milwaukee Braves.

He made his first of three All-Star teams and placed third in the National League Rookie of the Year balloting behind **Wally Moon** and **Ernie Banks**. (Henry Aaron came in fourth.)

Conley struck out the side in the 12th inning of the 1955 All-Star Game and was the winning pitcher. He won 28 games over the next three seasons, chipping in nine victories to the Braves' 1957 National League pennant cause.

He was traded to Philadelphia during the 1959 spring training and won a dozen games for the Phillies that year. The right-hander pitched two hitless innings in the All-Star Game, with strikeouts of Ted Williams and Yogi Berra.

Conley threw a three-hitter against the Cubs in August, turning in a complete game despite getting hit by a pitch on his pitching hand in the third inning, resulting in a season-ending fracture.

His 12–7 record and 3.00 earned run average for a last-place club earned him the Comeback Player of the Year Award. He was traded to

Boston after the 1960 season, giving Conley the distinction of playing for three major professional teams in the same city (Red Sox, Braves, and Celtics).

Arm problems that had plagued him since 1955 ended his baseball career late in the 1963 season.

STARTING IN 1962—**Tom Tresh**, Dean Chance, **Ken Hubbs, Dick Radatz, Jim Bouton**, Buck Rodgers, **Sam McDowell, Clarence "Choo Choo" Coleman, Donn Clendenon, Boog Powell**, Jim Fregosi, **Diomedes Olivo**.

Hubbs and Tresh were Rookies of the Year. Hubbs handled more than 400 consecutive chances at second base for the Cubs without an error and won a Gold Glove, while batting .260.

He visited children in hospitals and spoke to church groups. Opponents praised him for the kind of man he was. The February before what would be his third season, Hubbs died in a plane crash. At the age of 22.

Tresh was a versatile switch-hitter who was the Yankees' starting shortstop most of his first season. He hit 20 home runs (fifth-most on the '62 power-packed team) and drove in 93 runs.

Chance, who pitched 18 and one-third innings for Los Angeles in 1961, became the Angels' mainstay the next season. The right-hander averaged 265 innings over a five-year period.

In 1964, he was close to untouchable, allowing 194 hits in 278 innings and pitching 11 shutouts. A 20-game winner with a 1.65 ERA, he won the majors' only Cy Young award and placed fifth in MVP voting.

Sam McDowell threw smoke and a lot of pitches out of the strike zone. "Sudden" twice struck out more than 300 batters in a season in an era of much lower strikeouts than today and had 2,453 Ks in 2,492 innings over a 15-year big league career. A 20-game winner in 1970, McDowell led the American League in strikeouts six times and in bases on balls five.

Olivo was officially a rookie pitcher with Pittsburgh in 1962. But the left-hander had debuted with the Pirates in '60 at the age of 41, one year younger than **Satchel Paige** when he became the oldest first-time player in major league history. Olivo appeared in 62 games for the Bucs in 1962, saving seven with a 2.77 ERA.

ENDING IN 1962—Richie Ashburn, Bob Cerv, **Billy Goodman**, Wilmer Mizell, Clem Labine, **Granny Hamner, Wynn Hawkins, Turk Lown, Dave Philley, Gene Woodling,** Ed Yost, **Chuck Tanner.**

Ashburn was the quintessential leadoff hitter, reaching base nearly 3,800 times in 15 seasons. A .308 lifetime hitter with a .396 on-base percentage, "Whitey" scored 90 or more runs nine times. He had 14 triples for the 1950 Whiz Kids who took the National League pennant in a shocker.

The Hall of Fame center fielder reached base more than 40 percent of the time in six seasons and led the league in batting twice. Ashburn, a five-time All-Star, struck out as many as 50 times only once.

Hamner, another Whiz Kid, was a steady infielder who played 17 years in the majors. He batted .299 in 1954 with 63 extra-base hits, including 11 triples. The three-time All-Star had 21 home runs and 92 RBIs in 1953.

Mizell, the country boy who became a Congressman, was instrumental in Pittsburgh winning the 1960 National League pennant. After winning 69 games in six-plus seasons for the Cardinals, they traded him to the Pirates early in the '60 season and he won 13 for them. The southpaw was known as "Vinegar Bend," the name of a community near where he grew up in Alabama.

Woodling did not like being called "my left-handed-hitting left fielder" by Casey Stengel. He hated being platooned, but made the most of it, playing on five World Series champions in six years with the Yankees. Woodling hit .318 with three home runs in those Series, .284 with 147 homers overall in 17 big league seasons.

Tanner hit a home run for the Milwaukee Braves on the first pitch he saw in the major leagues, then hit 20 more in an eight-year career that ended with the Angels. He got only 89 at-bats over his last four seasons. Known for his eternal optimism, Tanner led four teams in a 19-year managerial run, taking the Pittsburgh Pirates to the World Series title in 1979.

LAST PITCH OF 1962 SEASON—Yankees Ralph Terry to San Francisco's Willie McCovey. As he had been two years earlier, the right-hander was touched for a rocket. But this one was a line drive right at New York second baseman Bobby Richardson. The Yanks won Game Seven of the World Series, 1–0, as Terry pitched a four-hitter in Candlestick Park.

Chapter 7

The Strategies, They Are A-Changin'

One major change that took place in the 1960s had nothing to do with rules. It was the emergence of the stolen base as a viable offensive weapon.

From the early 1930s until the '60s, base stealing was practically in moth balls. It had become pretty much an individual thing, with the team approach to aggressive basepath behavior laying dormant.

The Chicago White Sox shook things up in the 1950s, and out of necessity, made stealing profitable. And lethal. Following suit, several teams in both leagues dusted off the running game and made it a potent piece of their arsenals.

Al Lopez took over as manager of the White Sox in 1959 and took Chicago to the American League pennant. The club gained notoriety as the Go Go Sox.

The White Sox led the league in stolen bases almost annually, while ranking low in home run totals. Lopez made the most of what he had, turning Luis Aparicio and Jim Landis loose and finding ways to convert singles and walks into runs.

Aparicio led the AL in '59 with 56 stolen bases, while the White Sox led all of baseball with 113. Chicago hit only 97 homers. In the World Series, the Go Go Boys met the Los Angeles Dodgers, who topped the National League in steals.

Other teams took notice, and in 1960 there were more stolen bases in the major leagues than there were stolen base attempts 10 years earlier. The next season was the first in 18 years that big league teams combined to reach the 1,000 mark (1,046) in steals.

More than 1,000 were swiped collectively each year for the rest of the decade, and by 1969 the total of successful steals was approaching 2,000.

Little Looie and his White Sox continued running in the new decade and were joined in high octane high jinx by the Dodgers. Particularly Maury Wills, like Aparicio, a shortstop. Wills swiped an astounding 104 bases in 1962, while L.A. rang up 198 steals.

In setting a major league record, Wills stole more bases by himself than each of the other 19 *teams* totaled.

The big leagues had nearly 1,500 steals collectively in 1964 and '65, the total zooming to 1,850 in 1969, when six teams swiped more than 100 bases apiece.

In 1964, Aparicio reached a personal high of 57 steals, four more than Wills. The next season, Wills stole 94; meanwhile, a new rabbit was zipping around American League bases.

Bert Campaneris, still another shortstop, had 51 steals for the '65 Kansas City Athletics. Campaneris stole 50-plus bases five straight seasons, with a career-best 62 in 1968 and '69, the A's first two years in Oakland.

And, then, there was Lou Brock, a veritable stolen base machine for a dozen years, beginning in the middle of the 1960s and lasting well into the '70s. In that 12-year stretch, he averaged 65 stolen bases, with 118 in one season, 74 and 70 in two others.

National League pitchers must have thought Brock was born on second base. He sure perched on the keystone bag a lot during the three years in the '60s when St. Louis won the pennant.

In 103 games with the Cardinals in 1964 after they got him from the Cubs, he stole 33 bases and had 21 doubles. In 1967, he had 52 steals and 32 doubles. In 1968, he had 62 steals and 46 doubles.

Getting to second means being in scoring position, and Brock cashed in by averaging 105 runs over 10 seasons.

Brock, Wills, Campaneris, or Aparicio led the majors in stolen bases each year during the 1960s, with the exception of one. Seattle's Tommy Harper swiped 73 in 1969.

It is important to note that these players, and a handful more who put up impressive numbers, were not the only base thieves. Rather than an isolated practice by a small number of individuals, the practice of running on the pitch became a trend. Not a fad, mind you, but a trend.

It also should be pointed out that the stolen base did not replace the home run as THE weapon of choice. Balls continued to fly out of ball yards with about the same frequency, the per-team home run average very close to what it had been a decade earlier.

But stolen bases were way up in the 1960s as speed took its place beside power as keys to scoring runs. Baseball changed for the better, variety providing an entertaining spice which also proved successful.

The game was different, and the new style morphed into the baseball played today. More and more players on the move, more and more who steal bases AND hit home runs.

Players were more athletic, which translated into more overall speed, which led to more running. Managers would have been crazy to apply the brakes when they could get someone in scoring position without throwing away an out with a sacrifice bunt.

WHICH BRINGS US TO EARL WEAVER. When he arrived on the scene in Baltimore halfway through the 1968 season, he was a refreshing contrast to what had come to be expected of big league managers.

Weaver was like the good old boys, the way he could argue and give it to the men in blue. And he possessed the feisty mannerisms of Stanky and Leo and some of the others. It even seemed his approach was easy to understand: just sit back and wait for the three-run homer.

As it turned out, the feisty little man was much more complex. His ideas that appeared to go against "the book" made more sense than that book. The best example was The Earl's disdain for wasted outs.

Some reporters misinterpreted what the Orioles' manager meant by that. They wrote that he hated the sacrifice bunt. But that wasn't exactly true; in fact, Weaver's clubs frequently were first or second in the American League in sacrifices attempted.

What he preached against was giving away outs. The 27 outs each offensive team has at the start of a game, he reasoned, were its most treasured commodity. As a result, Weaver usually eschewed sacrificing early in a game or every time Baltimore had the tying run on first base in the late innings.

It was assumed, incorrectly, that he was happy just to sit back and wait for the long ball. Just slug it out with the other team. Nope, he just figured an out was better used to allow a hitter to hit than to order him to bunt and gift-wrap an out for the opponent.

Of course, Weaver certainly loved the home run. Who among managers doesn't? It's the quickest way of scoring. One swing of the bat can erase errors, as well as a deficit. But he did bunt. Just not every time a situation supposedly called for it.

"Supposedly" referencing all the games down through time that managers called for a bunt because managers before them had called for it. Weaver didn't necessarily go by the book; he wrote his own book.

Part of it involved platooning; or rather, platoon players. He got the most out of an entire roster. He gave players, particularly typically part-timers, the best chance to succeed by plugging them in where they could be successful.

A guy who might have been a pinch hitter and nothing more on another team would find himself in the lineup on certain days against certain pitchers.

Doing that kept everybody on the Orioles' roster sharp, while getting maximum mileage out of that roster.

GEORGE ANDERSON'S ROOKIE BASEBALL CARD was produced in 1959 by Topps, which also printed a card of the infielder in 1960. He did not even play that year. Not one bit.

After playing 152 games for the Philadelphia Phillies in '59, Anderson was gone from the big leagues. Little wonder, perhaps, looking at his stats for that season: a .218 batting average, .282 on-base percentage, and .249 slugging percentage.

No home runs, 34 RBIs. A second baseman, he made 12 errors in 758 chances. The Phillies finished in last place in the National League at 64-90.

Fast forward to 1970, when Anderson had re-invented himself as Sparky and had landed himself a brand-new job. Manager of the Cincinnati Reds.

That gig was definitely for him. The Reds won 102 games and the NL pennant that season. They finished in first place three times in his first four years, taking four pennants and two World Series titles in his first seven years as skipper.

One thing Anderson did, in addition to winning a lot of games, was to pay attention and learn. For example, although he came from an era when relief pitchers weren't held in high esteem, he put great trust in his bullpen.

Too much, if you asked the Reds' starting pitchers. They felt he lived on the top step of the dugout, ready to yank them from games. Not only ready, they believed, but anxious.

Sparky's propensity to change pitchers earned him the nickname Captain Hook. (and several other monickers from Cincinnati's rotation.)

LOOKING AT TODAY'S PITCH LIMITS and the idea of a starting hurler getting his team to the seventh inning and a bullpen of one-inning specialists, Anderson might been viewed as leaving his pitchers out there too long.

Statistics are an integral part of baseball. They reveal much about a player's contribution, his value. Before the RBI was included on the stat sheet, batting average was the main way to measure a hitter.

The RBI column showed that certain players could be quite productive despite an unimpressive batting average.

But the buggy might also drive the horse, so to speak. Statistics can influence how players are viewed in terms of their assumed importance.

There is no better example than the save. It called managers' attention to guys who at one time were used out of desperation or when a game got out of hand.

The save made relievers "somebodies," eventually leading to the modern-day Closer. The ultimate artiste who has become sheer royalty.

CROSLEY FIELD WAS THE SITE of major league baseball's first documented save, after it became an official statistic in 1969. Los Angeles Dodgers right-hander Bill Singer earned the save on April 7, 1969, in the season-opener.

Singer pitched three scoreless innings after taking over for Dodgers starting and winning pitcher Don Drysdale. Singer did not allow a hit, while walking one batter and striking out one, as the Dodgers downed the Reds, 3–2.

Jerome Holtzman is credited with changing baseball by his creation of the save statistic, but as he said, it was the managers who decided to hold back their best relievers for the end of the game.

Jerome Holtzman, a longtime sportswriter, invented the save in 1960 when he was covering the Cubs. Chicago had a very good bullpen duo in right-hander Jim Brosnan and lefty Bill Henry, neither of whom received much attention for the job they did in protecting leads.

Elroy Face, the little Pittsburgh relief pitcher, was indirectly responsible for the save becoming an official major league stat. He had an 18–1 record in 1959, with all of the decisions coming out of the bullpen.

In looking back at the '59 season, Holtzman noted that, of Face's 18 wins, 10 came after he had allowed the opponent to tie the score or go ahead, only to pick up victories when Pittsburgh scored in the late innings.

As a result of his 18–1, Face was lauded by many writers as the best relief pitcher in baseball, praise that was unfounded in totality since more than a won-lost record should have been considered. Holtzman pointed out that Face had been better in 1958, when his record was 5–2.

The only criterion, other than the wins and losses, for judging relievers was earned run average, and that was also not an accurate barometer since what happened to inherited runners was not reflected in a pitcher's ERA.

So, Holtzman came up with the idea of awarding a save to a relief pitcher who entered a game with the potential tying or winning run on base or at bat and who then finished the game without relinquishing the lead.

Holtzman presented his idea to Lou Boudreau, a Hall of Fame shortstop who was a Cubs broadcaster at the time. Boudreau liked it, and Holtzman proceeded to pass along his save proposal to J.G. Taylor Spink, the publisher of The Sporting News, the magazine that was known for so long as the Baseball Bible.

Spink also liked the idea of saves, and he began giving a trophy every season to the top reliever in both the American and National League. The first Firemen of the Year, chosen by The Sporting News in 1960, were the Cardinals' Lindy McDaniel and Mike Fornieles of the Red Sox.

The Baseball Association of America appointed Holtzman chairman of a group to propose to the committee for official scoring rules that the save be included in box scores and be made an official statistic. That did not happen until 1969.

For the nine previous years, Holtzman wrote a weekly Sporting News story in which he listed leaders in the race for the Fireman of the Year, including the save as an unofficial stat. When it was adopted, the save became the first new major statistic since the RBI was added in 1920.

Researchers went through old box scores to retroactively calculate saves. The save rule was amended in 1973 and again in 1975. Here are the current qualifications for a save: (1) the relief pitcher must finish a game won by his team and cannot be the winning pitcher; (2) he must enter the game with a lead of three or fewer runs and pitch at least one inning, or (3) he must enter the game with the potential tying run on base, at bat, or on deck, or (4) he must pitch at least three innings regardless of the score.

The latter provision has led to some laughable saves in which pitchers have mopped up lopsided victories and allowed several runs while lasting three innings.

The modern-day closer almost always comes into games in the ninth inning with no one on base, sometimes with a two- or three-run lead. Those situations are much more comfortable than most of the ones in which Roy Face and Hoyt Wilhelm normally found themselves.

Chapter 8

Cutback in Power

On January 26, 1963, members of the Major League Baseball rules committee met with an agenda to give pitchers a boost in an effort to quiet the storm of home runs. The result was a vote to expand the strike zone.

Until then, a pitch had been defined as a strike if it crossed the plate between a batter's armpits and the top of his knees. The new strike zone included the area from a batter's shoulders to the bottom of his knees.

Committee members noted that they were only returning the strike zone to the way it had been before 1950. However, a history check revealed that the strike zone at that time was from a batter's knees to his shoulders. The key wording was "from the bottom of the knees" as opposed to "the knees."

So, the new strike zone was not the old strike zone, but was larger—moving higher and lower.

Roger Maris' home run outburst was a definite factor in the rules being changed. Because of the Yankee right fielder's threat to the sacred record of Babe Ruth, an old friend of Ford Frick, the commissioner personally tried to make it harder to hit homers.

But that was just an underlying part of the motivation behind widening the strike zone and helping the pitchers. There was a feeling around baseball—again, originating with Frick—that offenses were too potent.

It was feared that offense was taking over the game, that too many runs were being scored, and that home runs had become cheap.

In 1962, 3,001 homers were hit in the major leagues, a record at that time. Frick, who even said he would like to see the spitball brought back, thought the balance between pitchers and hitters was out of whack and that pitchers were in desperate need of help.

Influenced by the Commissioner, the rules committee returned to what was called "the old strike zone." Adding an inch or two at the bottom of the strike zone would hopefully induce more ground balls, while producing fewer fly balls, therefore fewer homers.

From a hitter's standpoint, the new strike zone definitely made it tougher, particularly on lower pitches. "I could tell a tremendous difference," said George Altman, who batted over .300 in back-to-back seasons while playing for the Chicago Cubs.

"I am 6-foot-4, and they were calling pitches down at my ankles— very low strikes. The strike zone got bigger, and then it got exaggerated. That made it rough on us hitters, especially against guys like Gibson, Koufax, and Drysdale. They were tough enough as it was."

The desired result was attained immediately. In 1963, total runs scored decreased by 11.6 percent, while bases on balls issued in the majors dropped by 12.3 percent. Home runs fell by 9.9 percent.

The batting average for the National League dipped 16 points and it was eight points lower in the American League. Meanwhile, strikeouts increased by eight percent in the majors, pushing the ratio of the number of strikeouts to every walk from 1.6 in 1962 to 2.0 in '63. The majors' collective earned run average fell by exactly half of a run.

Runs, home runs, batting averages, and ERAs continued their downward spiral. League batting averages sank below .250 10 times (out of a possible 12) from 1963-68.

The period from 1963 until the early 1970s was known in baseball as the Second Dead-Ball Era.

The first, which lasted from 1901-1919, was characterized by offenses built around speed. There were few power hitters in the major leagues during that time, and home runs were almost non-existent.

Thirteen times during those two decades, a league leader in home runs hit fewer than 10. The 1908 Chicago White Sox, who finished 24 games above .500, had a .224 team batting average and a meager total of three home runs.

Huge ballparks encouraged offenses to bunt, hit and run, and steal bases, utilizing speed as their primary weapon. The same baseball was sometimes used for nearly 100 pitches in a game, and the spitball was legal, two more factors in the low scoring.

Pitchers' enormous overall success during the 1960s defied logic in one respect as four new teams were added early in the decade. Four more were added in the second shot of expansion, which took place in 1969.

Four expansion teams played most of the 1960s, meaning that anywhere from 40 to 50 pitchers were needed to stock those franchises.

Logically, expansion dilutes pitching because the additional pitchers would not be in the majors without the new teams. Of course, a few of the pitchers in question might prove to be very good, having only needed the opportunity to prove it.

Normally, though, more is less when it comes to the number of pitchers throwing in the major leagues. It stands to reason, then, that hitters would benefit from feeding off of expansion teams' pitching; at least, in the first few years of their existence. As a result, offensive numbers would figure to be bloated during that period as would earned run averages.

That, however, did not happen, a fact obscured by whopping numbers achieved by several hitters during the two initial years of expansion.

In 1961, Norm Cash batted .361, Roberto Clemente .351, and Elston Howard .348; Roger Maris hit 61 home runs, Mantle 54, Orlando Cepeda, Jim Gentile, and Harmon Killebrew had 46, and Rocky Colavito hit 45.

In 1962, Tommy Davis batted .346 and knocked in 153 runs; Willie Mays smacked 49 homers, Killebrew hit 48, and Hank Aaron had 45.

Such glaring offensive production was part of the reason the strike zone was widened prior to the 1963 season.

The American League first expanded in 1961, adding the Washington Senators and Los Angeles Angels.

In 1960, the eight American League teams hit a collective .255, while pitchers had a 3.87 ERA. In 1961, American League hitters had a .256 batting average, and it fell to .247 in 1963. The American League earned run average was 4.02 in 1961 and 3.63 in 1963.

National League expansion began in 1962, adding the New York Mets and Houston Colt 45s.

In 1961, the eight National League teams batted .262 collectively. In 1962, National League hitters combined for a .261 batting average, followed by .245 in 1963. The NL earned run average in 1961 was 4.03, dropping to 3.94 in the first year of expansion and a very good 3.29 in 1963.

The lower '63 statistics should not be misinterpreted to indicate that the additional pitchers forced into action by expansion necessarily improved the overall quality of pitching.

The conclusion, instead, is that the new strike zone was the reason for the drop in those numbers in 1963. Notice that batting averages and ERAs were down in both leagues the first year of the larger strike zone.

Back in 1950, the Major League rules committee shrunk the strike zone—from the batter's armpits to the top of the knees—and offenses flourished.

The best league earned run average for a season during that decade was 3.67, and league earned run averages shot up to 3.95 and higher 12 times. The big league batting average for the 10-year period was right at .260, and the 1950 Boston Red Sox hit .302 as a team.

Don Drysdale's huge frame, sidearm delivery, and willingness to pitch inside made him a very intimidating figure on the mound, especially for right-handed batters. (National Baseball Hall of Fame and Museum)

Another huge advantage for pitchers during most of the 1960s was a high mound. A 1950 rule set pitchers' mounds at a standard 15 inches, but there was no enforcement, and the mounds in some ballparks were extremely high.

Six-foot-six Don Drysdale and 6-foot-2 Sandy Koufax of the Dodgers comprised one of the most intimidating and most successful pitching combos in baseball history.

As formidable as they were, there were reports that they got some extra "home cooking" in Los Angeles, where the mound was built up particularly high. A glance at the pair's earned run averages tends to support the theory that something was up.

Koufax and Drysdale combined for earned run averages of 1.98, 2.01, 1.46, 1.89, and 2.01 in Dodger Stadium from 1962-66. Their combined ERAs on the road were more than a run higher in each of those five years, with the exception of 1963.

Altman, the only left-handed batter to hit two home runs in one game off of Koufax, felt the new rules had an effect on him. Stats support Altman.

After batting .318 and .303 and combining for 49 home runs and 170 RBIs in 1961 and 1962, he fell to .274 and .230 in 1963 and '64, with nine homers and 47 runs batted in each year.

"Some of those mounds looked like mountains," Altman said, laughing. "The one in Los Angeles seemed pretty high to me. Koufax would stand up there and throw that big overhand curve ball, and it just went straight down, like it was rolling off the table. Again, he had overpowering stuff and didn't need any help, but the higher mound made him practically unhittable."

The ballparks were also an important factor. During the 1960s, almost every park was pitcher friendly. The only real exception was Atlanta Fulton County Stadium.

Dodger Stadium in Los Angeles, the Astrodome in Houston, Cleveland's Municipal Stadium, New York's Shea Stadium, Oakland-Alameda County Coliseum in Oakland, Busch Stadium in St. Louis, and Candlestick Park in San Francisco all had ample foul territory that provided a lot of extra outs.

Home runs were harder to come by as fences were farther from home plate and the carry of the ball was not particularly good anywhere other than Atlanta and, for some day games, Shea Stadium.

Chicago's Wrigley Field has been a home run haven when the wind is blowing out, but it frequently blows in towards home plate, making it difficult to get a ball out of the park.

The increase in night games also helped pitchers. Batters do not see the ball as well under the lights, and the ball carries better in the daytime.

Fielders began using larger gloves, which meant more balls could be caught, thus improving defenses. More pluses for pitchers.

Despite the shift from power to pitching, 10 hitters clouted 250 or more home runs during the 1960s. Five (Killebrew, Aaron, Mays, Frank Robinson, and McCovey) hit 300 or more.

THE NEW YORK YANKEES went rather meekly into that good night of the 1963 World Series. The more accurate version is that they were tamed by Koufax and Company.

In sweeping the Yankees, Los Angeles pitchers held New York to 22 hits and four runs. The Dodgers only got 25 hits in the four games but made them count.

In addition to Sandy Koufax's two complete-game victories, fellow lefty Johnny Podres allowed one run in eight and a third innings and Don Drysdale pitched three-hit shutout.

Former Yankee first baseman Bill Skowron had a two-run single in Game One and a solo home run in Game Two. Catcher Johnny Roseboro clouted a three-run homer in Game One. The Davis Duo, Willie and Tommy, combined for five RBIs in the Series, and Frank Howard slugged a solo homer.

ALOU WAS A NAME found in major league box scores for many years and one that also is good for a couple of trivia questions.

Felipe was a three-time All-Star who batted over .300 three times and hit 20 or more home runs in four seasons. He hit 206 home runs with a .286 batting average in his 17-year career.

Matty, a two-time All-Star, led the National League in hitting in 1966 with a .342 average. A .307 hitter in a 15-year career, he had 231 hits in 1969.

Jesus compiled a .280 lifetime batting average over 15 years. His best was with Houston in 1970, when he hit .306.

All three Alou brothers were outfielders and they all came up with the San Francisco Giants. On September 10, 1963, they made history by batting consecutively in a game in a 4-2 loss to the Mets in the Polo Grounds.

In what was his major league debut, Jesus pinch hit in the eighth inning and grounded out. Matty then struck out, also as a pinch hitter. Felipe, batting in the leadoff spot for the Giants, grounded out.

Felipe Alou was the best all-around player of the 3 brothers, totaling more than 200 homers and 2000 hits in his career. He led the NL in hits, total bases, and runs scored in 1966. (National Baseball Hall of Fame and Museum)

Five days later, the Alou brothers made history again as the three of them comprised the San Francisco outfield in the eighth inning at Pittsburgh. Felipe was in center field, Matty in left, and Jesus in right.

STARTING IN 1963—Gary Peters, Jimmie Hall, Willie Stargell, Ron Hunt, Pete Rose, Mickey Lolich, Manny Mota, Pete Ward, Gates Brown, Rusty Staub, Jim Wynn, Bill Freehan, Tommy Harper.

Rose and Peters were Rookies of the Year. A left-hander, Peters won 19 games and had an American League-leading 2.33 ERA for the Chicago White Sox. He won 20 the next season and again led the league in 1966 with a 1.98 earned run average. He hit 19 home runs and batted .222 in his career.

Pops. That was what Stargell was affectionately known by in the Pittsburgh Pirates' clubhouse. He hit double-digit home run totals his first 18 full seasons in the majors and ended his Hall of Fame career with 475, hitting 48 in 1971 and 44 in '73.

In 1979, the 39-year-old Stargell swept MVP honors by winning the award in regular season (tie with Keith Hernandez), the National League Championship Series, and the World Series.

Harper was a speedy outfielder who broke in with Cincinnati, scoring 126 runs for the Reds in 1965. He made his biggest splash when he stole 73 bases for the Seattle Pilots in '69, the most steals in the American League since Fritz Maisel's 74 for the 1914 New York Yankees. Harper hit 31 home runs the next season for the Milwaukee Brewers and placed sixth in the AL MVP voting.

Mota and Brown were prolific pinch hitters. Mota had 150 career hits off the bench, while Brown rapped 16 pinch-hit home runs.

ENDING IN 1963—Stan Musial, Red Schoendienst, Jim Lemon, Frank Torre, Jim Brosnan, Dale Long, Early Wynn, Dave DeBuschere, Pumpsie Green, Whitey Herzog, Luis Arroyo.

Elijah "Pumpsie" Green, a 26-year-old infielder, was called up to the Red Sox in the middle of the 1959 season, making Boston the last major league franchise to integrate its roster.

Green recalled that before his first game, it was Ted Williams who asked if he would like to warm up. Their pre-game throw-and-catch sessions continued until Williams retired. The best of Green's five big league seasons was 1961 when he hit .260 with six home runs for the Red Sox.

Long set a major league record (since equaled by Don Mattingly and Ken Griffey Jr.) by homering in eight consecutive games for Pittsburgh in 1956. In '58, he became the first left-handed-throwing catcher in the majors in 56 years when he appeared behind the plate in two games for the Cubs.

Wynn was determined to get his 300th win. And the prospects of doing so were certainly promising after a 1959 season that saw the burly right-hander win 22 games and the Cy Young Award.

He was 39 then, and although he won 13 the next year, gout and a sore arm made pitching difficult. The White Sox cut Wynn in the spring of 1963. Cleveland, his original team, signed him in June, and on July 13, he notched No. 300 and a ticket to Cooperstown.

Lemon hit 141 home runs from 1956-60 He combined with Washington teammate Roy Sievers for 54 or more homers each of those five years, with a high of 66 in 1960 when Lemon hit 38.

Arroyo was a Cinderella story to be sure. He flopped around with three teams for parts of four seasons before discovering a screwball and success.

The little left-hander went 5-1 with a 2.88 ERA out of the Yankees' bullpen in 1960. He was unreal the next year, pitching in 65 games with a 15-5 record, a 2.19, and 29 saves. The magic left as suddenly as it appeared, his earned run average doubling in each of the next two seasons.

LAST PITCH OF 1963 SEASON—Dodgers Sandy Koufax to New York's Hector Lopez. Playing right field because Roger Maris was injured in Game Two of the World Series, Lopez hit a ground ball to shortstop Maury Wills, who threw to Bill Skowron at first for the out. It gave Los Angeles a 2-1 win at Dodger Stadium and a four-game sweep of the Series.

FIRST AND LAST—On October 12, 1963, the first and last Hispanic American major league All-Star Game was held in the Polo Grounds, the final baseball game played in that ballpark.

The National League team defeated the American League, 5-2, as a little over 14,000 people showed up. Showcase rosters included Roberto Clemente, Orlando Cepeda, Juan Marichal, Luis Aparicio, Minnie Minoso, and Vic Power.

Tony Oliva had two hits, including a double, and an RBI. Manny Mota went 2-for-2 and drove in two runs. Marichal pitched four innings of two-hit shutout baseball, but did not get a decision. **Al McBean** picked up the win as he threw four innings of shutout relief.

Chapter 9

African Americans Make Their Mark

Fourteen of the 32 players selected for the 1962 National League All-Star team were African American or Latin American. It was a sign of how far integration of Major League Baseball had come since Jackie Robinson took the field for the Brooklyn Dodgers in 1947.

The next year, his teammate, Roy Campanella, became the second African American to stand out in the National League, while Larry Doby became a standout player in the American League starting in the summer of 1947. The following decade saw a parade of African American players who quickly achieved star status. First Newcombe, then Willie Mays, Ernie Banks, Henry Aaron, and Frank Robinson and others.

An even larger wave of African American stars would emerge in the 1960s. Aaron, Mays, and Newcombe each won an MVP award, Ernie Banks took two, and Roy Campanella won three of them in the 1950s. Frank Robinson also established himself among baseball's elite players, while Wills, Roberto Clemente, Orlando Cepeda, and Willie McCovey began paving their roads to stardom with the dawning of the '60s.

Seven of the 10 National League Most Valuable Players in the 1960s were African American or Latino, and they were seven different players: Frank Robinson, Wills, Mays, Clemente, Cepeda, **Bob Gibson**, and McCovey.

This group of players captured the top four spots in the MVP voting two of those years and comprised four of the top five two other times.

Listing the top five players in each year's National League MVP voting to compile a total of 50 for the entire decade (even though some of the names were repeated), 29 of the names belonged to African American and Latino players.

This is a staggering number when considering that more than 80 percent of the major league players during the 1960s were white, meaning that a hugely disproportionate percentage of the African American and Latino players were stars, many of the super variety.

Almost every pennant-winning effort during the '60s was fueled by African American players, many of whom were just beginning to flirt with greatness. As the decade progressed, names like Marichal, Brock, Stargell, Morgan, and Gibson grew to be recognized.

By 1969, a large number of baseball's so-called household names—the superstars—belonged to African American and Latino players.

George Altman, a two-time National League All-Star, offered an opinion as to why so many African American players were standouts in the 1960s. "To tell you the truth, I believe we were just hungry," he said.

"African Americans did not have the opportunity to play major league baseball for a long time. When we did, we wanted to be exceptional. I'm not saying the African American players were hungrier than the white ones; it's just that we really wanted to take advantage of the chance we had.

"Mays, Aaron, Banks, Clemente, (Frank) Robinson . . ." Altman said. "You could see at first glance that they were great ballplayers. The thing with them was that they did it year-in and year-out; that's what makes a superstar.

"We had so many Hall-of-Fame guys in the 1960s. It was a gold mine. That's why I think that was such a special time. The major leagues had just mined the African American players, and they were coming to stardom.

"It is pretty amazing that so many of the stars and superstars were black players," Altman said. "A lot of it, I think, had to do with our backgrounds. Although we did not have the workout facilities many of the white players had, we had to work hard when we were growing up.

George Altman began his career in the Negro Leagues, made two All Star teams while with the Cubs, and hit more than 200 home runs in the Japanese major leagues.

"I chopped wood. It was something I had to do a lot of, and it made me stronger. It was kind of like training, only we didn't know it. We didn't have all of the weight lifting and trainers back then, but most of the African American players were strong."

During the 1960s, African American and Latino players won seven batting championships, all 10 home run crowns, and eight RBI titles in the National League.

Clemente won all of his four batting titles and led all big league hitters with a .328 average for the decade. Aaron, Mays, and McCovey led or shared the lead in homers three times apiece. In leading the entire major leagues in RBIs during the 1960s, Aaron drove in the most runs in the National League three seasons.

African American and Latino pitchers were one-two in big league wins for the decade, Juan Marichal recording 191 and Gibson 164.

American League African American and Latino players won four batting titles, one home run crown, and one RBI title during the 1960s.

African American and Latino stars did not appear on the American League horizon as soon or as frequently as in the National League. Perhaps NL owners and general managers felt pressure to keep up with the Dodgers, seeing that their willingness to sign those players was paying off in the win column.

In 1963, 15 years after it first happened in the National League, Elston Howard became the first African American to win the American League Most Valuable Player Award.

There was a bit of irony in that slice of history as Howard was a member of the New York Yankees, whose reluctance to sign African American players for so long may have influenced other American League teams and may have contributed to their demise in the latter half of the decade.

Just as National League clubs were influenced by the successful Dodgers, who aggressively pursued and added African Americans, American League teams might have figured they should follow the opposite path taken by the mighty Yankees.

Don Buford felt the fact that a large number of African Americans excelled in the big leagues during the 1960s was mainly a matter of just getting a chance.

He played 10 years in the majors, five with the Chicago White Sox and the last five with Baltimore. The Orioles played in three straight World Series with Buford playing left field and batting leadoff. He was selected to the 1971 American League All-Star team.

"Everyone knows there were many outstanding African American players a long time ago," he said, "but they didn't get to play. As to why so many of us were among the better players in the 1960s, I think you would get a better answer by talking to the major league owners and the scouts.

"You have to talk about baseball providing opportunities. In the 1960s, there was a whole racial situation going on, and that led to African American people getting more opportunities in many areas, not just in baseball."

Two players were the keys to major league fans accepting African American men wearing major league uniforms. One was the Liberator. The other was the Ambassador.

Jackie Robinson was the Liberator. He broke baseball's color barrier on April 15, 1947, when he ran onto Ebbets Field with the Brooklyn Dodgers as they played the Boston Braves.

He was 28 years old when he won the first Rookie of the Year Award ever given. He was the National League Most Valuable Player two years later when he won the league's batting crown. Robinson batted hit .311 over 10 seasons and stole home 19 times.

The Ambassador was Willie Mays. He came along four years after Robinson opened the door for African American players and was not even the first African American on his team, the New York Giants.

He oozed good will. Known as the "Say Hey Kid," Mays brought an unmatched exuberance to baseball. His wide smile, enthusiasm, and bubbly personality turned people from all walks of life into instant fans.

Altman hit 101 home runs in nine big league seasons, most of them with the Chicago Cubs. He hit a pinch homer in the first 1961 All-Star Game, and he joined Banks, Billy Williams, and Ron Santo to give the Cubs their own "murderer's row" for a couple of years.

Altman did not arrive in the majors until he was 26, having played college baseball and then in the Negro Leagues.

"I went to Tennessee State," he said, "and the business manager there was a friend of Buck O'Neill. Mr. O'Neill recommended that I try out for the Kansas City Monarchs.

"They were primarily a barnstorming team the year I played with them because most of the real good Negro League players had signed with major league teams," Altman recalled.

"Mr. O'Neill was also responsible for signing three of us at the same time with the Cubs. The others were Lou Johnson and **J.C. Hartman**.

"I played at Burlington, Iowa, in the minors. It wasn't too bad because Iowa was a little more liberal than a lot of states. But I did run into some problems along the way."

A native of Goldsboro, North Carolina, Altman knew all about racial prejudice. "I would get called some names in a few places, such as Quincy, Iowa, but when I got to the big leagues, I seldom heard any of that.

"Remember, by the time I came up (1959), it had been 12 years since Jackie Robinson got it started for us. Everything had died down by then.

"One thing I recall is that, initially, African American players were not allowed to stay at the same hotel in St. Louis with our white Cubs teammates. It was about two years before we were able to stay there (in the Chase Park Plaza Hotel).

"And even then," Altman said, "the people from the hotel told us African American players that they would let us sleep there, but they didn't want us going into the dining room. It was hard.

"I knew about stuff like that from growing up in the South, but it still grates on you. Things get on your mind and keep you from being relaxed, and that can affect the way you play ball.

"Even in dealing with teammates," Altman said, "you had a funny feeling . . . you knew most of them actually condoned that sort of thing; they thought that separating whites and African Americans was the right way to do it.

"We had one or two white guys, though, who would have stayed with us African American players if they could have. They saw the way things were done as unfair, and they didn't like it."

It is interesting that the first four teams—the Dodgers, Indians, Giants, and Braves—to use African American players would also be the first four clubs to reap immediate and extensive rewards from their contributions.

The Dodgers, Giants, and Braves combined to win nine of the 10 National League pennants in the 1950s. One of those three teams won every flag from 1951–59 after the Philadelphia Phillies' Whiz Kids won it to start the decade.

Larry Doby, who played 10 years in the majors and twice led the American League in home runs, helped Cleveland win pennants in 1948 and 1954. Doby was the second African American to play in the major leagues, and the first in the American League. Doby first appeared with the Indians on July 5, 1947 and dealt with some of the same maltreatment and prejudice as did Jackie Robinson in the NL. Doby was elected to the Hall of Fame in 1998, but never received anywhere near the notoriety of Robinson for his trailblazing efforts.

There was an unspoken quota system regarding African American players during the 1950s. By the middle of the decade, three—and sometimes four—of Brooklyn's eight position players were African Americans.

Third baseman Robinson, second baseman Jim "Junior" Gilliam, and catcher Campanella were almost always in the starting lineup. They were frequently joined by left fielder Sandy Amoros.

That was a private concern of the Dodgers' front office brass, who felt having too many African American players would not bode well at the ticket windows.

Brooklyn's front office was not the only one to think that way as there seemed to be a consensus to hold the number of African American players to a minimum.

The quota notion disappeared from the majors in the 1960s. Anxiety over percentages was over-ridden by the desire to put the best players on the field, and an increasing number of the best players were African Americans.

From 1960–82, the National League won 23 of 26 All-Star Games, including seven straight and 11 of 13 (with a tie) in the 1960s.

An All-Star Game MVP was named for the first time in 1962, with Maury Wills the recipient. African American and Latin players took home 14 of the first 21 awards.

The American League's slow start in signing African Americans was still having a noticeable effect when the decade opened, as a total of only 22 were used by the league's eight teams in 1960, while 65 African Americans played for National League clubs the same year.

In 1969, however, 75 African Americans played for the American League teams, and 101 appeared in games for clubs in the National League. There were 12 teams in each league by then, but an increase of more than 100 percent was was still significant.

Equally telling is a look at starting lineups in the middle of the decade. In 1964, 38 African American players were starters on a regular basis in the National League and 16 in the American League.

It was not until September 1, 1971 that a major league baseball team started a lineup consisting of all African American or Latin American players. On that day, at Pittsburgh's Three Rivers Stadium, Pirates manager Danny Murtaugh penciled the following names onto his lineup card to face the Philadelphia Phillies:

Rennie Stennett 2B
Gene Clines CF
Roberto Clemente RF
Willie Stargell LF
Manny Sanguillen C
Dave Cash 3B
Al Oliver 1B
Jackie Hernandez SS
Dock Ellis P

Fourteen African American players helped the Pirates to win the National League pennant and the World Series title that season — 24 years after Jackie Robinson's historic first major league game.

Chapter 10

1964: Hot Corner MVPs and Two Old Knucklers

The 1964 Minnesota Twins proved that no matter how many you hit out, you've still got to get 'em out. They smashed 221 home runs, with six players hitting 20 or more. Harmon Killebrew led the Twins and the American League with 49, the fourth straight year and the fifth in six that he eclipsed 40. **Bob Allison** and **Tony Oliva** hit 32 homers apiece, Jimmie Hall had 25, **Don Mincher** 23, and **Zoilo Versalles** 20.

Minnesota's muscle was further reflected by 494 extra-base hits, 737 runs scored, and a .427 slugging percentage. As for getting outs, Twins pitchers posted a 3.58 earned run average and committed 145 errors, the fifth-lowest and second-most in the league, respectively.

The result was a 79–83 record that left Minnesota in sixth place in the American League standings, 20 games out of first.

BOB GIBSON'S DOGGED VICTORY over the New York Yankees in Game Seven of the 1964 World Series is well documented. How he pitched with two days rest, and how, despite not having his best stuff, he persevered with heart and determination.

What Gibson did to get St. Louis to the Fall Classic is among the big stories of the season. Starting August 24, with the Cardinals 10 games behind in the National League standings, he threw seven consecutive complete games, three on short rest. In the last six weeks of the season, Gibson went 9-2.

For the Yankees, the '64 Series was their last hurrah of the decade. It would be 12 years before they would return to the World Series and 13 before they would win another one.

When the Pinstripes fell, they fell hard . . . and far. New York finished eight games under .500 and 25 games out of first place in 1965, then plummeted into last place in '66.

While the Yankees were headed downward, things were just the opposite for the Cardinals. 1964 marked a return to prominence as they made their first World Series appearance in eighteen years.

Two decades earlier, the Cardinals were ruling the roost, and their 1946 Fall Classic was their fourth in five years. The 1964 resurrection triggered the same sort of run for St. Louis, which played in three Series in five years during the '60s.

Ken Boyer drove in 90 or more runs for seven consecutive years, culminating with 119 in his 1964 MVP season. (National Baseball Hall of Fame and Museum)

THERE IS NO CLEAR AGREEMENT ON what the qualifications should be for a Most Valuable Player. Some voters say the winner of the award should be the player who meant the most to the team that won the pennant. Others feel the MVP is the best player, the one who had the best season.

The old saying "We coulda finished last without you" suggests that big numbers for a bad team do not make a player valuable. Lesser stats for a pennant winner mean much more.

In 1964, a pair of third basemen were the MVPs. On the surface, one was an obvious choice, while the other's selection raised a few eyebrows if not questions.

Ken Boyer was a logical choice as the National League MVP after knocking in 119 runs and scoring 100 for the first-place Cardinals. But Willie Mays (wasn't he always in the conversation?) slammed 47 home runs and kept the Giants in the pennant race.

But Boyer drove in more runs, and when viewing the total picture, he was probably the most deserving. He was the most valuable player on the best team in the league.

One of the criteria for choosing an MVP should be not just what he did but when he did it. And that is where we find perhaps the Cardinal third sacker's biggest "value" in 1964.

Going into September, St. Louis was seven and a half games out of first place. The rest of the way, the Cards went 22–10 to win the flag by a game. Boyer drove in 26 runs in those 32 games. Clutch runs to be sure.

He hit seven home runs, adding six doubles and three triples in that crucial stretch. Oh, and he didn't miss a game all season, playing all 162.

BROOKS ROBINSON HAD THE BEST overall season for the American League team that was the best for the longest in 1964. Baltimore eventually finished in third place, while its third baseman grabbed eighteen first-place MVP votes, and with Mickey Mantle getting the other two.

Playing 163 games, Robinson enjoyed career bests with 194 hits, 28 home runs, 118 RBIs, and a .317 batting average as well as .368 and .521 on-base and slugging percentages, respectively.

One particular stretch reflected his ability to come through when the Orioles needed him most. From July 28 through August 28, he clouted 11 home runs and drove in 28 runs. He kept Baltimore in the thick of an extremely tight race, the Birds going from a game behind to a half-game ahead over the thirty-two days.

It was business as usual on defense as Robinson won his fifth straight Gold Glove on the way to his winning 16 in a row.

THE 1964 ST. LOUIS CARDINALS were an interesting bunch, to put it mildly. No fewer than 14 of the most prominent members of the '64 World Series championship roster landed in St. Louis via the transaction route, which at the time was rather unusual.

Five of the eight regulars were acquired in trades. First baseman Bill White from the Giants, both second baseman Julian Javier and shortstop Dick Groat from the Pirates in separate deals, center fielder Curt Flood from the Reds, and left fielder Lou Brock from the Cubs.

St. Louis also grabbed starting pitcher Curt Simmons off the scrap heap. The left-hander, one of the Whiz Kid stars, won 115 games for the Phillies before experiencing arm trouble that limited him to 10 innings in 1959. Philadelphia released him two days before his 31st birthday, St. Louis signed him on May 20 of 1960, and Simmons went on to win 18 games as the Cardinals won the 1964 National League pennant.

Catcher Tim McCarver, third baseman Ken Boyer, and right fielder Mike Shannon were the St. Louis everyday players who were signed by the Cardinals.

Seven of the everyday players, Shannon being the exception, were All-Stars at some point in their Cardinal careers. So was ace pitcher Bob Gibson, who collected about every trophy possible for his line of work. The quintessential "crafty lefty," Mike Cuellar, who went on to a fabulous career with Baltimore Orioles, won five games and saved four others for the Cards.

Ken Boyer was one of seven brothers to play professional baseball. Clete, also a third baseman, was a sensational fielder who played 16 years in the majors. Cloyd pitched five years in the big leagues, four with the Cardinals. Wayne, Lynn, Ron, and Len played in the minors.

McCarver, Shannon, and Uecker became better known as broadcasters than as players. Uecker, far better.

He first rode his infamy to fame, guest-hosting on late-night television, his schtick essentially making fun of his own ineptitude. The highlight of his career, he boasted, was a walk-off sacrifice fly in an intersquad Spring Training game. Movies and television followed, and then Uecker settled in as a broadcaster for the Milwaukee Brewers, a job he has now held for 47 years.

McCarver had a distinguished major league career, which lasted 21 years. He was an All-Star catcher and finished second behind teammate Orlando Cepeda in voting for the 1967 National League MVP Award. He has been a nationally acclaimed television sportscaster.

White also spent time behind a microphone and later served six years as the president of the National League. Joe Morgan—the other Joe Morgan—who was briefly on the St. Louis roster in '64, went on to manage in the major leagues as did Bob Skinner and Roger Craig.

Craig had known extreme success and failure, playing for perennial pennant contender Brooklyn and for the annual cellar-dwelling New York Mets. He served the '64 Cards as a dependable swing-type pitcher, making 19 starts and coming out of the bullpen 20 times. Working 166 innings, Craig was 7-9 with five saves and a 3.25 earned run average.

Red Schoendienst is one of the best-loved Cardinals ever. He helped St. Louis win World Series championships as a player, coach, and manager. A member of Johnny Keane's 1964 coaching staff, the redhead was a 10-time All-Star second baseman who played for the 1946 Cards and the '57 Milwaukee Braves, both of whom won it all.

Taking over as skipper following the '64 season, Schoendienst guided St. Louis to National League flags in 1967 and '68, with the Cardinals winning the World Series in '67. A Hall of Fame player, he managed St. Louis 12 seasons and parts of two others, totaling over 1,000 wins.

Schoendienst replaced Keane, who took the Cardinals to the '64 World Series championship, only to switch sides. Less than 24 hours after St. Louis had defeated the Yankees in Game Seven, Keane resigned as manager.

Bing Devine had been the Cardinals' general manager since 1957. He swung the deals that brought White, Brock, Javier, Flood, and Groat (among others) to St. Louis.

But Devine wasn't even around when the Cardinals celebrated their regular-season comeback that netted the 1964 pennant and then the World Series title.

He was fired by team owner Gussie Busch on August 17, with the Cards nine games out of first place. It was believed Busch was not only dissatisfied with the club's performance, but that he also felt his GM had lost control of the team. Bob Howsam replaced Devine, who was a good friend of Keane.

DICK GROAT HAD A KNACK FOR PLAYING on teams that won pennants and World Series. The shortstop played a vital role for both the 1960 Pirates and the '64 Cardinals.

Traded from Pittsburgh to St. Louis after the 1962 season, he finished second in the MVP voting in his first year as a Cardinal, his best all-around season.

A nine-year veteran at the age of 32, Groat had 201 hits, a league-leading 43 doubles, 11 triples, and drove in 73 runs, while batting .319 with a .377 on-base percentage.

He was part of the entire Cardinals infield to start in the 1963 All-Star Game. The shortstop joined first baseman Bill White and third baseman Ken Boyer in being voted by their peers to start for the National League.

When Pittsburgh second baseman Bill Mazeroski was unable to play because of an injury, Julian Javier of the Cardinals took his place.

1964 SAW THE FULL-TIME ARRIVAL of two great players who enjoyed two of the best rookie seasons in baseball history—Tony Oliva and Richie (Dick) Allen. Both had Hall of Fame talent, but both have come up short on that honor (so far at least), though they both have advocates for that cause, especially Allen.

Baseball writers sometimes made a big deal of Dick Allen's artwork around first base. While playing there on defense, he would pass idle time by doodling in the dirt with his spikes. Writers cited it as a sign of Allen being eccentric.

But one opposing pitcher said, "I know exactly what Allen is doing. He's mapping out how he's going to destroy me—and and every other pitcher—the next time he comes to bat."

If that was the case, Allen followed through on many of those plans, because he destroyed a lot of pitchers. In 15 major league seasons, he smacked 351 home runs, batted .292, got on base 38 percent of the time and slugged .574. His OPS+ of 156 (an OPS that is 56% better than average) is 20th all time, which ties him with none other than Willie Mays and Frank Thomas, one point better than Henry Aaron, Joe DiMaggio, and Mel Ott!

When he first came up with the Phillies, Allen played third base. After four years, he was shifted to left field for a season and settled at first base. Of course, Allen's best position was always hitter. He turned out offense in a variety of ways. Power was the obvious, as he cracked 30 or more home runs six times, topped by 40 in 1966. Over his career, 41 percent of his hits went for extra bases.

Allen produced, driving in 90 or more runs six times, topped by 113. He had double-digit stolen base totals a half-dozen times, with a high of

20 and 133 in his career. He possessed enough speed to leg out 10 or more triples his first four seasons.

He played seven seasons in Philadelphia, moving to St. Louis in a seven-player trade after the 1969 season. Thirty-four homers and 101 RBIs weren't enough reasons for the Cardinals to keep Allen, and they swapped him to Los Angeles.

The Dodgers also kept him a year before dealing him to the Chicago White Sox, and Allen was the American League MVP his first of three seasons with them.

BOB WEILAND was a left-handed pitcher who bounced around the major leagues for 12 years. His lifetime record was 62–94, but for three glorious seasons, he was a winner with the St. Louis Cardinals.

"Lefty" won 41 games for the Cards from 1937–39, with a career high of 16 in '38. They weren't winning pennants in those days, but memories of the Gas House Gang still lingered in St. Louis.

They were played out by a group of Cardinals players who formed the Mudcat Band in 1937. A photograph from that year portrays five Cardinals in their baseball uniforms, pretending to play music with bats and gloves as their instruments.

Weiland is among them, "playing" his glove. Holding the mitt to his mouth, the pitcher appears to be blowing into it as if he was playing a harmonica.

PHIL LINZ WOULD HAVE FIT right in with that bunch of Cardinals. Except he could have played his harmonica instead of his glove. Yogi Berra probably wished Linz had come along in the 1930s rather than 1964.

It was August 20, and the Yankees had been swept in a four-game series in Chicago, leaving New York four and a half games behind the White Sox in the American League standings. The mood was somber on the team bus to the airport.

At least, Berra thought it should have been. When he heard Linz playing his harmonica in the back of the bus, the Yankees' manager was livid and told the infielder to stop.

Linz, upset at not being used more (he was hitting .259), threw his harmonica and shouted. He complained that he was being singled out by Berra despite the fact that he was not playing enough to be contributing to the losses.

Linz was fined. Berra, for his part, demonstrated that he was in charge of his team—something that had been questioned by the Yankees' front office.

New York charged back to win the pennant, finishing a game ahead of the White Sox. But after the Yankees lost to the Cardinals in the World Series, Berra was fired.

It was believed the Linz Harmonica Incident added fuel to a fire the team's management had already built. It helped them believe what they were already feeling: that Berra had lost control of his team.

Linz, by the way, played shortstop for the Yankees in the 1964 Series, replacing **Tony Kubek**, who had injured his wrist in late September when punching a door after striking out.

Linz batted .226 in the Series and hit two home runs. He lasted one more season with the Yankees and played out a mediocre seven-year career in 1968 with the Mets.

STARTING IN 1964—**Dick Allen, Wally Bunker**, Tony Oliva, **Tommy John, Jim Ray Hart, Rico Carty, Luis Tiant**, Jesus Alou, **Willie Horton, Denny McLain**, Don Buford, Mike Cuellar, Wes Parker.

Rookies of the Year were Allen and Oliva. Allen, known as Dick and Richie, had 201 hits, 80 of them for extra bases, scored 125 runs, and batted .318 for the Phillies that year.

He averaged 29 home runs over his first 11 seasons and was the 1972 American League MVP when he slugged 37 homers and had 113 RBIs and a .420 on-base percentage for the White Sox.

Tiant always had pizzazz. Sporting a Fu Manchu mustache that became his trademark, he used a windup in which he completely turned his back to batters, and following big wins, he could be seen with a large grin and a larger cigar. El Tiante won 229 games, including 20 or more four times.

John is an interesting Hall of Fame omission. Compare his lifetime 288–231 record and 3.34 earned run average with HOF member Ferguson

Jenkins' 3.34 and 284–226. Jenkins had nearly 1,000 more strikeouts, while John had a 6–0 edge in post season wins.

The lefty is perhaps best known for the surgery named for him. He was the first pro athlete to have the procedure, which replaces an elbow ligament with a tendon from another part of the body.

Hart seemed to hit every ball hard. He belted 31 home runs and drove in 81 runs as a 22-year-old San Francisco Giants rookie. He averaged 28 homers and 89 RBIs over his first five years. Hart never had more than 13 homers or 53 RBIs his last six seasons.

ENDING IN 1964—Gus Bell, **Don Hoak, Don Elston**, Sam Jones, **Charlie Maxwell**, Billy Pierce, **Paul Foytack, Pete Runnels**, Duke Snider, **Billy Bruton**, Art Fowler, Bobby Shantz.

Known as both "Toothpick" and "Sad Sam," Jones was an extremely talented pitcher who seldom had much offensive or defensive support. The right-hander with the big curve ball pitched in the Negro Leagues before reaching the majors at the age of 25.

Jones was the first African American to pitch a no-hitter, throwing one for the Cubs in 1955. He went 14–20 that year, and despite five seasons of losing 13 or more games, he was 102–101 for his career.

Wildness was always a problem. He led the National League in both strikeouts and walks three seasons. Jones' finest year was 1959 when he had a 21–15 record with a league-best 2.83 ERA.

"Sunday Charlie" was what they called Maxwell. The popular Tigers outfielder earned the nickname when he hit home runs in four successive trips to the plate in a Sunday doubleheader against the Yankees in 1959. Also known as "Paw Paw," Maxwell smacked 120 homers for Detroit from 1956–60.

Bruton was a fleet-footed center fielder for the Milwaukee Braves in the 1950s and Detroit Tigers in the early '60s. Bruton led the senior circuit in stolen bases his first three years, and accumulated 1,651 hits in his career, despite not breaking into the majors until he was 27 years old.

Runnels won two batting titles and is nearly as famous for finishing second to teammate Ted Williams in 1958. A three-time All-Star and .291 lifetime hitter, Runnels managed as many as 10 home runs once in 14 years. Runnels clearly was a better hitter than baserunner, as he also, incredibly, was thrown out on all 13 of his stolen base attempts in his first two years in the majors, and had only a 42 percent success rate in his career.

Pierce won 211 games in an 18-year career, helping the Chicago White Sox and San Francisco Giants win pennants. Twice a 20-game winner, the left-hander posted a 1.97 earned run average in 1955. He pitched six shutouts that season and had seven in '53.

LAST PITCH OF 1964 SEASON—Cardinals Bob Gibson to New York's Bobby Richardson. The second baseman, who had 13 base hits in the World Series, popped out to St. Louis second sacker Dal Maxvill. Gibson and the Cards won Game Seven in Busch Stadium, 7–5.

Chapter 11

Plenty of Primo Pennant Races

The 1960s boasted a number of thrilling pennant races. Several went down to the last day of the season. Another lasted beyond that. One sensationalized what was called "The Big Choke," which overshadowed what was also a Colossal Comeback. Both in the same year.

1962—Arch-Enemies Battle Beyond Last Day

The National League race was a scriptwriter's dream. The arch-enemy Dodgers and Giants battled from opening day until the final game of the season . . . and even longer.

San Francisco won 10 in a row and 12 of 13 to build a four-and-a-half-game lead over Los Angeles on May 20. The Dodgers then reeled off 13 straight wins to grab a half-game edge on June 8. L.A. stayed on top most of the month before the Giants slid back in front by a half-game entering July.

The Dodgers shut out San Francisco behind Sandy Koufax on July 8 to grab a half-game lead, and they remained in first place for 84 days. Until the very last day of regular season.

When the Giants caught them.

Trailing by four games on September 22, the Giants won three straight to close within two games. San Francisco then split its final four games, while the Dodgers dropped their last four, making it 10 of their final 13.

Holding a one-game edge on the final day, Los Angeles was shut out by the Cardinals' **Curt Simmons**, 1–0. The Giants nipped Houston, 2–1, on Willie Mays' eighth-inning home run.

And they were tied. Both teams finished with records of 101–61, necessitating a best-of-three playoff between bitter enemies. What could be better?

Game One went to the Giants in rollicking fashion, 8–0. They knocked out Sandy Koufax—he was on the brink of winning another Cy Young Award—after one inning—and hit four home runs on the day. Two by Willie Mays. Lefty Billy Pierce threw a three-hitter.

That was in Candlestick. The next day, it was a different ballpark and a different story. The Dodgers scored seven in the sixth and one in the bottom of the ninth for an 8–7 survival triumph.

They hit five singles, two doubles and no home runs off eight San Francisco hurlers, including **Gaylord Perry**, who retired the only batter he faced in the final inning. Eight walks and one error by the Giants helped the Dodgers stay alive.

In an oddity, the Dodgers' two key offensive achievements in the ninth occurred without an official at-bat. **Darryl Spencer**, pinch-hitting for Duke Snider, laid down a sacrifice bunt that moved runners to second and third. After an intentional walk, **Ron Fairly's** sac fly plated the deciding run.

Home for the rubber game, the Dodgers took the lead on Tommy Davis' two-run homer in the sixth and added insurance an inning later on a "Maury Wills home run," which amounted to a single by the shortstop, a steal of second and third, and a trot to the plate when Giants catcher **Ed Bailey** threw the ball into left field.

4–2 L.A., and that's how it stood in the top of the ninth. Reliever **Ed Roebuck** remained on the mound after pitching three shutout innings. He escaped a bases-loaded-no-outs scare by throwing a double-play ball in the sixth and threw another in the eighth.

San Francisco's comeback was seasoned liberally by the Dodgers, who issued four bases on balls in the ninth and sprinkled in a wild pitch and their fourth error of the game. A pair of singles was the Giants' meager contribution to their four-run comeback rally.

Pierce pitched the ninth and was as masterful a finisher as he had been a starter. The Dodgers went down 1–2–3, closing their season in the worst kind of way: Losing to the Giants, blowing a lead in the final inning, and seeing the pennant slip out of their unsure hands.

1964—Old Guys Refuse to Knuckle Under

A pair of old knuckleballers figured prominently in both 1964 pennant races, each of which was decided by one game after going down to the final weekend.

Hoyt Wilhelm and Barney Schultz were closers, though the designation was not used back then. They were the guys responsible for getting the last outs of a game while protecting a slim lead.

That might have meant three outs, it might have been seven or eight. The reward was satisfaction and maybe a pat on the back. There was no save statistic. (Although saves were added to official game box scores retroactively.)

It was the thirteenth year in the major leagues for Wilhelm, the old master of the bullpen, who turned 42 years of age during the '64 season. He was pitching for the Chicago White Sox, his fifth big league team.

The right-hander from North Carolina had made his mark for hitting a home run in his first at-bat in the majors, for throwing a no-hitter while in the Baltimore Orioles' rotation, and for possessing one of the best knucklers in baseball.

Whereas Wilhelm was established, certainly one of the premier relievers in baseball, the 38-year-old Schultz was far from it. And yet, he went from oblivion to being the late-inning man down the stretch for the St. Louis Cardinals.

Signed by the Phillies in 1944, the right-hander languished 11 years in the minors before making his first major league roster at the age of 28. That was with the Cardinals on opening day, 1955, but after compiling a 7.89 earned run average in 19 games, he was sent back down.

Barney Schultz was 37 years old when he found lightning in a bottle for the 1964 Cardinals. A year later, he was out of baseball for good.

Schultz did not pitch again in the majors until 1959, when he appeared in 13 games for Detroit. His next stop was Chicago, where he chalked up a dozen saves in two seasons before the Cubs traded him back to St. Louis in June of 1963.

The Cardinals' manager was **Johnny Keane**, who was the skipper of the Cards' Omaha Triple-A team when Schultz pitched there in 1956–57. St. Louis used him 24 times in '63, then placed him on waivers.

Schultz began the 1964 season at Triple-A Jacksonville and did not allow a run in his first 28 appearances. At Keane's urging, Schultz was called up to St. Louis on July 31.

For the Cards, did not allow an earned run until late August and entered September with a 0.86 ERA. In the season's final five weeks, Schultz notched 12 saves, as St. Louis erased a four-game deficit to edge Philadelphia and Cincinnati by a game for the National League pennant.

Schultz pitched in 30 of the Cardinals' last 60 games and 16 in the last month, including five straight. He saved all five of those late September games, while working seven scoreless innings. His save on the final day of the season was his fourteenth. He finished with a 1.64 ERA in 49.1 innings.

Wilhelm was another late arriver. He was 29 when he began his rookie season in 1952, one in which he would pitch in the second-most games (71) of any year in his career. He went 15–3 with a 2.43 and 11 saves for the New York Giants.

Wilhelm went six years and more than 400 appearances before making his first major league start. He pitched in 1,070 games over a 21-year career ended when he was 49 years old. Many of his 228 saves were multiple innings, and he often entered a game with runners on base.

"Old Sarge" was a nickname from World War II days when he was awarded the Purple Heart. Also called "Old Folks" when he wasn't even near retirement, Wilhelm was tireless and durable for the White Sox in 1964. He came out of the bullpen a career-high 73 times and finished 55 of those games.

Wilhelm pitched 131.1 innings, earned 27 saves—his most ever—with a 12–9 record and an ERA of 1.99, the first of five consecutive seasons under 2.00, all when he was in his forties.

With the Sox battling to get back into the race after falling four games behind with only eight games remaining, the old knuckleballer was at his best.

He appeared in five of seven games, posting two wins and three saves and not allowing a run, while pitching two or more innings in six straight outings.

Throwing in both ends of a doubleheader against Kansas City, Wilhelm pitched four shutout innings in saving the first game and put up another zero to win the second.

The White Sox won their last nine games, but came up one game short of the New York Yankees. Wilhelm gave up one earned run in thirteen September outings, covering 29.1 innings.

Baltimore, Chicago, and New York see-sawed back and forth between first and third place in the American League. Hank Bauer's Orioles were atop the standings longer than anyone else.

The Birds either led or shared the lead for ninety-one days in 1964, having first place to themselves for seventy-three.

Baltimore stayed in first for a month, from June 14 through July 14, and held at least a share of the lead all but one day of August. The Orioles' last time atop the standings was September 18, when they were tied for first place.

Al Lopez's White Sox were in first place for 16 days and were tied for the lead an additional sixteen. Chicago's last outright lead was by a half-game on September 6, and its final share of the lead was 10 days later.

New York owned a half-game lead for one day in June and had at least a piece of first place the last six days of July. The Yankees did not regain sole possession of first again until September 19, and they kept it the rest of the season.

The Pinstripes of Yogi Berra won eleven in a row down the stretch and 13 of their last 14. They homered in 10 of those victories, Mantle and Maris going deep four times apiece.

In late June, Hank Bauer's Orioles put together a seven-game winning streak that catapulted them into a four-and-a-half-game lead over the Yankees, with the White Sox dropping six back.

Then, in mid-July, it was Chicago's turn to surge. Nine wins in an 11-game stretch pulled Al Lopez's club within a half-game of the lead. But in the end, it was the Yankees who prevailed … again.

AS PAINFUL AS IT WAS to watch, no discussion of the 1964 baseball season and pennant races could be complete without mention of the Philadelphia Phillies. THOSE Phillies. The ones infamous for The Collapse.

The Philly Phlop, Phold, or Phizzle.

And, there is no talking about that without considerable criticism of **Gene Mauch**. Generally regarded as an outstanding strategist and wily situational innovator, he is remembered for panicking down the stretch in '64.

"The Little General" did his best work with teams that were vastly undermanned, inspiring pennant pushes that fell short but won accolades for accomplishing so much with so little talent.

But when he did have the horses, they came up short. Or, in the case of 1964, Mauch went to the whip a bit early or too often with a couple of his thoroughbreds.

Maybe that is a tad harsh. Maybe not.

Certainly The Meltdown of '64 was not all the manager's fault. After all, in losing 10 straight, the Phillies were outscored 65–34, outhit 121–75, getting six or fewer four times, and they committed 13 errors.

All of those numbers, however, are overshadowed by Mauch's decision to pitch his two aces, right-hander **Jim Bunning** and lefty **Chris Short**, on two days' rest after Philadelphia's losing streak had reached six.

After absorbing a loss to Milwaukee on September 24, Bunning took the mound September 27, again against the Braves. They pounded him for 10 hits and seven earned runs in three innings of a 14–8 Phillies loss.

The next day, Short started with two days' rest and gave up seven hits and three earned runs over five and a third innings in a 5–1 loss in St. Louis.

Bunning was back on September 30 and was hit hard once more. The Cardinals knocked him out in the fourth inning after he surrendered eight hits and six runs, five earned.

That was the last of the 10 consecutive losses, dropping the Phillies two-and-a-half games out of first place. Before the plunge began, they led the National League standings by six-and-a-half games.

On the last day of the season, with the Phillies out of the race, Bunning pitched with three days' rest. He threw a six-hit shutout in Cincinnati for his 19th win. Bunning threw a dagger into the Reds, who finished a game behind St. Louis, but it was small consolation.

Philadelphia's two big hitters can't be faulted. Both were productive during the losing streak. Dick Allen batted .414, including .429 with five RBIs with men on base. **Johnny Callison** hit .275, including .400 with seven RBIs with men on base. Four of Callison's 11 hits during the streak were home runs, while six of Allen's 17 hits went for extra bases.

It is unfair to put the blame on Bunning and call him a choker, despite his two horrendous starts during the fatal losing streak. Both came with two days' rest.

Still, Short also had two starts with short rest. On September 25, he pitched seven and a third innings, allowing two earned runs, and did not get a decision. On September 28, he took the loss after lasting five and a third, giving up seven hits and three earned runs.

It's always easy to second-guess, but skipping **Art Mahaffey** in the rotation is a head-scratcher. He was the losing pitcher in the game that started the epic slide. It was a 1–0 loss to Cincinnati on September 21 as Mahaffey pitched six and two-thirds innings.

He pitched next on the 26th and did a creditable job, allowing three earned runs in seven innings. Two good starts in 10 games, while Bunning had one good one and two terrible starts in that span.

Who knows what would have happened had Mauch not rushed Bunning and Short back onto the mound? The easy response is that things could not have been worse. That does not, of course, mean they would have turned out better.

Everyone knows the second guess is always easier than the first. It's just that when a team is apparently cruising toward a pennant and falls apart, fingers are always going to point.

Most of them in 1964 pointed to Gene Mauch.

The Phillies ended in a tie with Cincinnati for second place, a game behind St. Louis. The Cardinals' comeback was itself quite a story. They played tremendous baseball over the last two-thirds of the season.

Trailing by 11 games on August 24, they played .718 baseball for nearly six weeks (winning 28 of their last 39 games) to capture the pennant. It went back farther than that, though.

A game under .500 on July 24, the Cards went 46–21 the rest of the way. A .687 winning percentage over more than two months. A colossal comeback, indeed.

1965 — Arms War Decides National League Race

The Giants and Dodgers were back at it again. A couple of other teams made brief runs, but as the dog days turned to the final days, it was just those two old rivals.

Milwaukee held a half-game lead on August 20, then lost eight of nine. Cincinnati was tied for first place on September 1, but lost seven of eight when the heat was on. Los Angeles was in the lead, tied for it, or within a game of it until the second week of September.

Then San Francisco, which had been kind of hanging around, got hot. Red hot. The Giants inched into first place by a half-game on September 8 and added to their lead. Eight days later, they owned a 14-game winning streak and a lead of four and a half games.

San Francisco homered in 12 of the 14 victories, hitting a total of 16 during the surge. Willie Mays smacked seven of those long balls on his way to a career-high 52, with Willie McCovey and Jim Ray Hart adding four apiece.

The Giants held onto first place until September 28, when they were overtaken by Los Angeles, which picked the perfect time to run off its own long winning streak. The Dodgers won 13 in a row and 15 of their final 16 games of the season, finishing two games ahead of San Francisco.

While the Giants did it with power, L.A. did it with pitching, the old Dodgers' standby. Hitting the fewest homers (78) in the National League in 1965, they threw 23 shutouts. Eight of them came during the Dodgers' closing victory stampede, and they allowed just one run in four other of those games.

During Los Angeles' torrid stretch, Sandy Koufax and Don Drysdale both notched four wins, and Koufax added a save. All of the left-hander's wins were complete games, and three were shutouts as he pitched 30 consecutive scoreless innings.

In Koufax's last four starts of the season, he allowed one run and struck out 51 in 36 innings. Remarkably, he blanked Cincinnati on two hits September 29, then threw a complete game at Milwaukee October 2. As clutch as it can get.

The Dodgers' 3–1 win that day clinched the National League flag. Working with two days rest, Koufax was as brilliant as ever in earning his 26th victory. Drysdale won 23 and batted .300 with seven home runs and 19 RBIs. Both pitched more than 300 innings.

1966 — Giants-Dodgers Déjà Vu

It was deja vu all over again . . . hey, just had to get Yogi's quote in here somewhere. For the third time in the decade, the Giants and Dodgers were the principal protagonists in the chase for the National League flag.

The Pirates made lots of noise, too, and actually sneaked ahead of the pack for a brief period at the start of September. Pittsburgh stayed close and finished close, three games out of first place.

San Francisco took the lead on May 5 and kept it until June 11, then returned to the top spot in the National League two days later, remaining there until July 17.

The Giants were tied for first place fifteen days during August, fell two game behind September 2, and never caught up despite winning their last six games of the season.

Los Angeles dropped six and a half games out of the lead the first day of July and pulled into a tie for first place the last day of the month.

They didn't stay there long. Falling as far as four games back, the Dodgers did not occupy the top spot again until September 11. Using a strong finishing kick (20–9 for the month), this time they stayed there for good.

The '66 National League pennant race boiled down to eight days. On September 9, Pittsburgh led San Francisco by a game and a half, with Los Angeles two games behind.

The Dodgers, enjoying a 16-game home stand, won eight in a row to go up by three and a half on September 16. Igniting the surge was some miraculous pitching, as the Dodgers threw four straight shutouts at the Houston Astros.

Claude Osteen tossed a three-hitter and singled in a run. **Al Ferrara's** pinch single drove in the game's only run in the eleventh inning as Don Drysdale and **Phil Regan** combined on a four-hitter. Sandy Koufax allowed six hits, and three pitchers gave up seven in another 1–0 victory that completed the sweep of Houston.

Meanwhile, the Giants were dropping five of eight games and the Pirates were losing four of six.

The title wasn't decided until the final day, Sunday, October 2. Trailing by one and a half games, San Francisco needed to win at Pittsburgh and for the Dodgers to get swept in a doubleheader at Philadelphia.

Those results would leave the Giants a half-game back and would necessitate playing a make-up game still remaining on the Giants' schedule.

The Giants beat the Pirates and the Phillies downed Los Angeles in the first game. But then Koufax took care of business.

Exactly as he had done a year earlier, the Swami of Southpaws nailed down the Dodgers' pennant with a marvelous performance on two days' rest.

On September 29, Koufax threw a four-hitter and struck out 13 in a 2–1 win at St. Louis. In the regular season finale, he shut out the Phillies for eight innings before settling for a 10-strikeout, 6–3 victory, his 27th.

Los Angeles put on a season-long pitching workshop. Its team earned run average of 2.62 was nearly a half-run lower than the next-closest staff.

Buoyed by Koufax, Claude Osteen, and 21-year-old **Don Sutton**, the Dodgers allowed 490 runs (3.02 per game), 87 fewer than the second-stingiest National League team.

1967 — The AL's Frenzied Four-Team Finish

This one was a real doozie! Four teams—Boston, Minnesota, Detroit, and Chicago—had a good shot at the pennant even in late September, and all four had sole possession of first as late as August 23. On September 6, the four were in a virtual tie for first. The White Sox and Twins were both 78–61, while the Red Sox and Tigers were a single percentage point behind at 79–62.

All of the contenders had their streaks. The Red Sox won 10 in-a-row in July and seven straight in August. The Twins won eight straight in July and seven in a row in August. The Tigers won seven straight in July, then lost the next seven. The White Sox won 10 in a row in May and lost their last five of the season.

Chicago was a game and a half back with three games left to play. Detroit trailed by a half-game entering the final day, with Boston and Minnesota tied for first.

Boston was in sole possession of first place for just five days prior to the final day of the season. The Red Sox's biggest lead was a game-and-a-half on August 30, and that lasted for only one day.

The Red Sox did not climb above .500 for good until the middle of July and had trailed by as many as seven games in early June.

The season came down to the last two days. On the morning of Saturday, September 30, Minnesota led Boston by one game and Detroit by one and a half.

The Tigers were home for back-to-back doubleheaders with California. The Twins were in Boston

Carl Yastrzemski's WAR of 12.5 in 1967 is the best by a position player since Babe Ruth in 1923. (National Baseball Hall of Fame and Museum)

for two single games with the Red Sox.

Detroit and California split both days. The Red Sox edged the Twins Saturday, 6–4, as Harmon Killebrew and Carl Yastrzemski both hit their 44th home run. Yaz went 3-for-4 with four RBIs.

The pennant was still undecided on Sunday, the last day of the schedule, with the Twins and Red Sox squaring off for what amounted to the American League championship game.

A pair of aces were on the mound, 20-game winner Dean Chance for Minnesota, 21-game winner Jim Lonborg for Boston.

Carl Yastrzemski went 4-for-4 and knocked in two runs as the Red Sox won the game and the American League pennant, 5–3. In the eighth inning, his throw from left field cut down Bob Allison trying to stretch a single into a double. Yaz's 7-for-8 over the last two critical games is undoubtedly history as one of the greatest clutch performances in baseball history.

1969—Two Different, but Equally Thrilling, NL Races

One ended up close, one didn't. But both National League divisional races that closed the decade had a certain electricity to them.

The 1969 season was the first to feature four sub-pennant races, with both 12-team leagues split into two divisions. The division winners in the two leagues then played best-of-five series to determine actual pennant winners that faced off in the World Series.

THE AMAZIN' METS—Incredibly inept in their early years, the New York Mets were feverishly hot down the stretch of the 1969 season. They won 36 of their last 46 games to take the National League East Division title by eight games.

A runaway, except that it wasn't. The Chicago Cubs led the National League East standings for 155 days before growing as cold as the Mets were hot. The Cubs faltered in September when they lost 17 of their last 25 games.

The rise of the Mets was nothing short of amazin'. They were in only their eighth year of existence and had never won more games than they lost in a season. They were just two years removed from the National League basement, a place the club occupied five of its first six years. New York escaped to ninth place in 1966 and climbed that high again in 1968, the first year Gil Hodges was the manager.

The Mets had been a bad joke for quite a while. The way they played made people both laugh . . . and hold their noses. The inaugural 1962 record of 40–120 was followed with 51–111, 53–109, and 50–112. A .299 winning percentage for four years.

The first hints that New York might be headed in a different direction were barely noticeable. Players like **Cleon Jones**, **Ron Swaboda**, and **Bud Harrelson** arrived quietly in the mid-1960s. **Tug McGraw** broke in in 1965, making nine starts and compiling a record of 2–7, though he had a solid ERA of 3.32.

Jerry Grote established himself as the first-string catcher in 1966 and batted .237, while Swoboda manned left field and Jones center. Jones hit .275 and stole 16 bases. A 19-year-old kid pitched three innings, absorbed a loss, and fanned six batters. He was **Nolan Ryan.**

A left-handed pitcher named **Gordie Richardson** wore jersey No. 41 for the Mets. He got into 15 games and compiled an 0–2 record and a 9.15 earned run average with one save.

In 1967, that number was on the back of Tom Seaver, not long before being dubbed Tom Terrific. Deservedly so. He went 16–13 with a 2.76 ERA, pitched 251 innings, and took home the Rookie of the Year trophy. A lefty, **Jerry Koosman**, made three starts and was 0–2.

Gil Hodges arrived in 1968. As New York's manager, but he had been there before, returning to the Mets after being one of the team's originals back in 1962. All but 361 of Hodges' 370 career home runs were hit as a Met.

New York had traded Hodges to the Senators in '63 so he could manage them, and they were 321–444 during his five years in Washington.

The former Brooklyn Dodgers' slugger knew how to win, and he was just the right man to teach the young players the Mets had assembled.

Seaver called Hodges the most influential person in his baseball career. The 1968 Mets eased into ninth place with a franchise-best 73–89 record.

New additions included Tommie Agee, a speedy center fielder, power-hitting part-timer Art Shamsky, and a slick fielding utility infielder named Al Weis.

1969 was the first major league season of division play. The Mets were in the National League East. So was St. Louis, which had played in back-to-back World Series.

The Chicago Cubs made themselves the team to beat. They were 22 games above .500 and owned a nine-game lead on June 15, and it was the same two months later. The Cubbies were up five games after a September 2 win in Cincinnati. Then the roof caved it. They lost their next eight games and 11 of 12. The month was disastrous for Chicago, which dropped 17 of 25 games.

The Mets, meanwhile, caught fire. They won 10 in a row and 13 of 14, then had another winning streak of nine games. New York went 23–7 in September, with Seaver and Koosman both going 4–0 for the month. The Mets finished the season with 100 victories, eight games ahead of the Cubs.

That was the second part of amazin', that New York—a game under .500 on June 1—came from so far back to win the East going away.

THERE WAS A THREE-TEAM FIGHT in the West. San Francisco, Cincinnati, and Atlanta were within an arm's reach of each other as the final full month of the season unfolded before the Braves took charge.

They won their last 10 games of September to finish three games ahead of the Giants and four up on the Reds. Atlanta's strong finish (20–6 in September) and ability to win the close ones (28–17 in one-run games) made the difference.

Cincinnati stayed in the battle with an offense that led the National League in runs scored (798) and home runs (171). **Lee May** hit 38 homers, one more than Tony Perez, Johnny Bench adding 26 and **Bobby Tolan** 21.

San Francisco had a nice balance—fourth in the league in both earned run average and runs scored—as Juan Marichal and Gaylord Perry combined for 40 wins, and Willie McCovey slammed 45 homers.

The Giants were on top of the standings as late as September 22 before losing three of four, while Atlanta was burning.

A couple of knuckleballers were instrumental in the Braves' run to the title. Phil Niekro won 23 games with a 2.56 ERA, while Old Reliable Hoyt Wilhelm provided extra push out of the bullpen for the short haul.

On September 8, the Braves acquired Wilhelm from the California Angels. Atlanta gave up a pair of outfielders, one of them a 20-year-old speedster named **Mickey Rivers**, who had hit over .300 that summer for Magic Valley in the Pioneer Rookie League.

Wilhelm was in his 18th major league season and, at age 47, he threw one of the hoppingest knucklers of all time. He would not be eligible for the post season. The Braves just wanted Wilhelm to help them get there. Which he did.

Appearing in eight games, he finished seven with a 0.73 earned run average. During Atlanta's key September winning streak, Wilhelm saved two games and won two.

Six of the Braves' 10 wins during their clinching streak were over last-place San Diego and three came at Houston. Two of the victories were nine-inning jobs by 18-game winner **Ron Reed**. Three came from Niekro.

The third, on September 30 against Cincinnati, gave Atlanta a two-and-a-half-game lead with one game remaining. Match, set, division title to the Braves.

THE PENNANT was then decided with a best-of-five series that was all Mets. And after their arms carried them to the brink of the National League flag, the Mets' bats led the way in the first-ever National League Championship Series.

New York's 2.99 earned run average was second-stingiest in the National League (behind the Cardinals' 2.94) in 1969. The Mets' run total of 632 was ninth out of 12 teams.

But Tom Seaver and Jerry Koosman were both roughed up in Atlanta. Seaver was touched for two homers and five earned runs in seven innings in the opener. Koosman, who was staked to an 8–0 lead, could not last long enough to get the win in Game Two.

Five unearned runs off Phil Niekro allowed the Mets to prevail in the first game. Home runs by Tommie Agee, **Ken Boswell**, and Cleon Jones were among 13 hits New York racked up off six Atlanta pitchers the next day.

The Mets completed the three-day sweep in front of more than 54,000 fans at Shea Stadium as their bats stayed hot. Agee and Boswell again hit home runs, as did **Wayne Garrett**. Half of New York's 14 hits were for extra bases. Nolan Ryan pitched seven innings of three-hit relief and fanned seven for the win.

Hank Aaron homered in all three games, adding two doubles along with seven RBI.

The New York Mets were going to the World Series.

Chapter 12

1965: A Rivalry Rages and Indoor Baseball

Much National League history has to do with the Dodgers and Giants. Brooklyn and New York. Los Angeles and San Francisco. East Coast. West Coast. It has been one of baseball's greatest rivalries. Easily the most heated.

The Giants and Dodgers have battled through many a September with their eyes on the National League pennant. Twice they ended with identical records, tied atop the standings.

Bobby Thomson's storybook three-run home run gave the New York Giants the pennant in 1951. The blast came in the bottom of the ninth inning of the third game of a best-of-three playoff with the Brooklyn Dodgers. The Giants rallied for four runs to win, 5–4.

In 1962, the Giants again came from behind with four runs in the ninth in the decisive third game of a playoff. Again, it was against the Dodgers.

August 22, 1965, to borrow a phrase, is a date that will forever live in baseball infamy.

The Dodgers were visiting Candlestick Park, sitting in first place in the National League standings, a game and a half ahead of their despised San Francisco rival. The mound matchup pitted future Hall of Famers Sandy Koufax and Juan Marichal. Koufax was 21–4, Marichal 19–9.

Maury Wills led off the game with a bunt single. When he batted in the second inning, Marichal knocked him down. In the bottom of the inning, Koufax fired a fastball over the head of Mays.

Marichal sent Ron Fairly diving to the ground in the top of the third. At that point, plate umpire Shag Crawford said, "Enough!" and warned both teams that the next close pitch would result in ejection.

Dodgers catcher John Roseboro, knowing Koufax wanted to even the score in terms of players biting the dust, took care of the matter himself. When Marichal led off the bottom of the third, Roseboro zipped a return throw to the mound very near Marichal's face.

Claiming later that the ball nipped his ear, Marichal turned and got into a cursing exchange with Roseboro before raising his bat and hitting the catcher on the head. Never before or since has one player hit another with a bat during a major league game.

Both dugouts and bullpens emptied as total chaos erupted. Mays played peacemaker and has been credited with defraying further injuries. Crawford tackled Marichal, who continued swinging his bat.

Roseboro required 14 stitches. Marichal was thrown out of the game. His penalty, considered mild by any standard, was eight game days (10 with off days) and a $1,750 fine.

Koufax, apparently shaken, walked two batters later in the inning and gave up a three-run homer to Mays. The Giants won, 4–3.

The Los Angeles lefty lost his next two starts but finished strong to go 26–8. Marichal missed two starts during his suspension, then went 3–4 in his last nine outings to end 22–13 with a 2.13 ERA.

The Dodgers won the 1965 National League pennant, finishing two games ahead of the Giants.

The Astrodome required 2,150 tons of steel—just for the roof.

THE EIGHTH WONDER OF THE WORLD. That was the billing given to the Houston Astrodome, the first domed sports stadium.

It was the a longtime dream of Judge Roy Hofheinz. The former Houston mayor headed a group that was awarded the major league expansion franchise in 1961 when they promised to build a covered stadium.

That was considered an absolute must for a big league team in Houston because of the city's extremely hot summers and the accompanying high humidity.

Construction began on the project in 1962, with the Astrodome opening April 9, 1965, when the New York Yankees and Houston Astros played an exhibition game. Houston had changed its nickname after being called the Colt 45's prior to the new ballpark being available for a major league season.

President Lyndon Johnson and his wife, Lady Bird, were on hand for the game, won by the Astros, 2–1. Mickey Mantle had the first hit in the Dome, a single, and also cracked the first home run.

The Astros opened the 1965 regular season at home on April 12, losing to the Phillies, 2–0. Left-hander Chris Short pitched a four-hitter, striking out 11, while Dick Allen provided the offense with a two-run homer off Bob Bruce in the third inning.

At first, the stadium had real grass, but it died and was replaced with artificial grass known as Astroturf. An oddity, a piece of broadcasting history, occurred in the Astrodome a couple weeks later. The New York Mets came into town for for a two-game series with the Astros.

After Houston won the first game, someone from the Mets suggested on the second day, April 28, that Lindsey Nelson, their play-by-play announcer, should broadcast from a gondola that hung more than 200 feet in the air above second base.

Nelson, the man with the sports coats of many colors, agreed, reportedly saying that he had survived World War II and three years of watching the Mets, so why not? (Nelson had served with the Ninth Infantry Division, "The Old Reliables," during the war.)

So, the gondola was lowered, Nelson and an engineer climbed in, and ascended 208 feet above ground. He did two innings of play-by-play, becoming the first man to announce a game within the field of play.

Casey Stengel was the Mets' manager, and with him on hand, a funny story was to be expected. Following is the one published in numerous newspapers:

As the game began, managers and umpires met at home plate to go over the ground rules. As the discussion wrapped up, Stengel turned to Tom Gorman, the crew chief, who was to work home plate that night.

"What about my man up there?" Stengel asked.

"What man?" Gorman said.

"My man Lindsey," the Old Perfessor said. "What if the ball hits my man Lindsey?"

Gorman looked up at Nelson, 208 feet above him, and said, "Well, if the ball hits the roof, it's in play, so I guess if it hits Lindsey, it's in play, too."

"How about that?" Stengel replied. "That's the first time my man Lindsey was ever a ground rule."

FELIX MANTILLA was an unlikely All-Star.

Before he arrived in Boston, anyway.

For years, his greatest notoriety as a big league baseball player was that he collided with Billy Bruton, ending the 1957 season for the Milwaukee Braves' center fielder.

In the first inning of a July game at Forbes Field, Pittsburgh leadoff hitter **Bill Virdon** lifted a pop fly into short center field. Mantilla, playing shortstop for Milwaukee that day in the place of **Johnny Logan**, went out. Bruton came running in from center. They rammed together hard.

A pair of Braves helped Mantilla hobble off the field, while Bruton was carried off on a stretcher. Mantilla was out for a while before coming back to finish the season.

Bruton underwent knee surgery and did not play again until the next year, missing the World Series in which Milwaukee beat the Yankees.

Mantilla was with the Braves six years, playing second, short, third, and in the outfield. He never managed more than 274 plate appearances, seven home runs, and a .257 batting average.

Chosen with the No. 12 pick in the National League expansion draft, he became one of the original New York Mets and enjoyed somewhat of a breakout season in 1962. Playing in 141 games, 95 at third base, Mantilla hit .275 with 11 homers and 59 RBIs.

In December, the Mets sent him to Boston for three players. He saw sporadic action his first season with the Red Sox, then became sort of a utilityman regular in 1964. Spending time at six positions in 133 games, Mantilla hit 30 home runs and batted .289.

He became Boston's everyday second baseman the next year and was selected to the American League All-Star team. Mantilla was hitting .316 with 12 homers and 59 RBIs at the break. He hit four home runs the rest of the way to finish at .275–16–89.

Mantilla's career lasted just one more year. He hurt his shoulder during the '66 spring training, was traded to Houston, and spent a month on the disabled list. After 151 plate appearances with the Astros, he asked for and received his release. He signed with the Cubs, tore an Achilles in spring training, and his career was over at the age of 32.

Finding Fenway friendly, Mantilla did enjoy his time in the spotlight, highlighted by being a 1965 All-Star.

SATCHEL PAIGE was the starting pitcher for the Kansas City Athletics on September 25, 1965. At the age (as close as anyone could guess) of 59.

The oldest pitcher in major league history, according to the record book, he pitched three shutout innings against the Boston Red Sox, allowing only a single by Carl Yastrzemski, while striking out one and walking no one.

The walking-no-one part was normal for Leroy, which was his actual first name. Legend has it he more than once demonstrated his pinpoint control by throwing pitches over a book of matches designated as home plate.

Accustomed to being called into games abruptly, he required just a pitch or two to get warm, saying he was always loose and ready to pitch. He pitched in the Negro Leagues for decades, frequently appearing in games day after day.

Paige turned 42 years old during his major league rookie season of 1948. He compiled a very impressive 6–1 record and a 2.48 earned run average, including three complete games, two shutouts, and a save, for the American League pennant-winning Cleveland Indians.

At age 45, he went 12–10, throwing 138 innings for the lowly St. Louis Browns in 1952, pitched another 117 at age 46 in 1953, then was out of the big leagues until his three-inning goodbye of 1965.

In 476 career innings, Paige was 28–31 with a 3.29 ERA.

THE MINNESOTA TWINS won their first American League pennant after moving from the nation's capital in 1961. Ironically, the Twins' clinching victory came in D.C. against the Washington Senators.

The franchise had not won a league title since 1933 when the Senators finished seven games in front of the New York Yankees. Washington was led that year by 26-year-old player-manager Joe Cronin, the shortstop and seven-time All-Star.

The '65 Twins took over first place July 1 and did not relinquish it. That, despite losing slugger Harmon Killebrew to injury August 2 and not getting him back until the middle of September. Limited to 113 games, Killebrew hit 25 home runs, the only time in a nine-year span he didn't get at least 31.

Three other Twins had 20 or more homers, Tony Oliva drove in 98 runs and Jimmie Hall added 86 RBIs. League MVP shortstop Zoilo Versalles had 76 extra-base hits, stole 27 bases, scored 126 runs, and knocked in 77. Jim "Mudcat" Grant won 21 and pitched six shutouts.

Tony Oliva was an American League All Star his first 8 seasons, and likely would be in the Hall of Fame were it not for crippling knee injuries that took a huge toll on his productivity after his age-32 season. (National Baseball Hall of Fame and Museum)

STARTING IN 1965— **Marcelino Lopez, Frank Linzy,** Joe Morgan, **Curt Blefary, Catfish Hunter, Jim Lefebvre,** Ron Swoboda, Phil Niekro, **Nelson Briles, Glenn Beckert, Rico Petrocelli,** Tug McGraw.

Rookies of the Year were Blefary and Lefebvre.

Voting for the National League honor caused some head-scratching. Lefebvre received 14 of 20 votes after batting .250 for the pennant-winning Dodgers. He hit 12 home runs, scored 57 runs, and had 69 RBIs.

Morgan, like Lefebvre a second baseman, got four votes. He batted .271 with 14 homers and 40 RBIs hitting leadoff and second most of the season. Morgan scored 100 runs and drew 97 walks for the Astros, who finished ninth.

Blefary batted .260 and hit 20 homers for the Orioles. Lopez won 14 with a 2.93 for the Angels.

Niekro was a 26-year-old rookie. The knuckleballer worked in relief until becoming a starter in 1967, when he led the National League with a 1.87 ERA. He was three-time 20-game winner and two-time 20-game loser, doing both (21–20) in 1977.

"Knucksie" was 40 then and went on to notch 100 additional victories, finishing with 318 at the age of 48. He spent 20 of his 24 years with the Braves, 18 in Atlanta. The Hall of Famer, who pitched more than 5,400 innings, was one of the nicest guys in baseball.

Petrocelli spent all 13 of his major league seasons with the Red Sox and is tenth on their all-time home run list with 210. He smacked 97 in a three-year span, including 40 in 1969. A shortstop his first six seasons, he played third base the last seven.

Jim Hunter was not called Catfish because he was a country boy from North Carolina, although he was just that. Kansas City Athletics owner Charlie Finley thought his young pitcher needed a catchy nickname, and that's how it came about.

Hunter was a tremendous big-game pitcher, keying three straight Oakland A's World Series championships and pitching for two more Series winners with the Yankees. He threw a perfect game, won 200 games by the time he was 30, and was a 20-game winner five successive years in the 1970s.

The Hall-of-Fame right-hander died from ALS when he was 53.

ENDING IN 1965—Yogi Berra, **Vic Power**, Roy Sievers, Dick Donovan, Nellie Fox, **Harvey Haddix, Don Mossi, Johnny Blanchard**, Tony Kubek, Don Zimmer, **Frank Lary**, Wally Moon, Ryne Duren.

Fox struck out just 216 times in more than 10,000 plate appearances. ONCE out of every 48. Never whiffing more than 18 times in a season, the Hall of Fame second baseman struck out 11 times in 698 trips to the plate in 1958—one time in every 63. You knew old Nellie was going to lay that big bottle bat on the ball.

Lary was the Yankee Killer. The Detroit right-hander never had an explanation, but he often had the Yanks' number. In 1958, he won 16 games, seven of them against New York.

A two-time 20-game winner for the Tigers, Lary had a 27–10 record vs. the Yankees from 1955–61, with 28 of his lifetime 128 victories over the Pinstripes.

Power never struck out more than 35 times in a season and was a superb first baseman. He won seven straight Gold Gloves, but was called a hot dog because he was a flashy player. Good enough, though, to be a four-time All-Star and finish in the top 20 in MVP voting three times.

Sievers was a very good player on some very bad Washington Senators teams. The 1949 American League Rookie of the Year went on to hit 318 home runs, smashing 21 or more nine straight seasons. In 1957, Sievers batted .301 with 42 homers and 114 RBIs.

Moon was the 1954 National League Rookie of the Year with the St. Louis Cardinals and clouted 24 home runs for them three years later. Traded to the Dodgers, he became famous for his Moon Shots—home runs he lofted to the opposite field in Los Angeles Coliseum.

Using an inside-out swing, the left-handed hitter served several of his 19 home runs over the 42-foot left-field screen in 1959. (251 feet to the foul pole.) Moon batted .302 and had 11 triples for the pennant-winning Dodgers, earning fourth place in the MVP voting.

LAST PITCH OF 1965 SEASON—Dodgers Sandy Koufax to Minnesota's Bob Allison. He got the Twins' left fielder swinging, giving Koufax 10 strikeouts in the Los Angeles 2–0 win in Game Seven of the World Series. It was played in Minnesota's Metropolitan Stadium.

Chapter 13

Boring Ball Yards Are Born

Ballparks. Ball yards. Diamonds. Ball fields. All names for the places baseball games are played. Hard-core fans once even thought of their favorite stadiums as tabernacles.

Not so much anymore. Not after the "cookie cutter" stadiums began to be erected. As they went up, the personality that was so much a part of old-time stadiums – and of baseball itself – disappeared into heaps of rubble.

The New York Yankees moved into Yankee Stadium in 1923 after sharing the Polo Grounds with the Giants the previous 10 years. The Giants built the last of four ballparks called the Polo Grounds in 1911 and stayed there until they departed for San Francisco.

The stadium, which was built between Coogan's Bluff and the Harlem River, was known for its unusual configuration and dimensions. Shaped like a bathtub, the Polo Grounds measured 279 feet down the left field line, 258 to right, and 483 to center, with power alleys of 449 and 450 feet.

In 1913, the Dodgers moved into brand new Ebbets Field, a place that became a cozy home ballpark for loving fans of "dem Bums." It was comfortable; everybody felt close to the action.

Walter O'Malley, a businessman who dealt primarily in real estate, purchased enough shares to become the Dodgers' majority owner in 1950. He looked around for land to build a new ballpark because Ebbets Field was getting old, and the crowds attending games there were getting smaller.

The word tabernacle is appropriate because so many of the old ballparks were viewed in a somewhat sacred context in the 1950s. None more so than Ebbets Field. It was a shrine.

Located in the Flatbush section of Brooklyn, it was the place people from all walks of life came together to not just cheer for, but embrace, their beloved Dodgers. The ballpark was not only the home of the Dodgers; it was home for their fans as well.

O'Malley said he would build a large parking lot on the land, along with a new ballpark. But he could not change the mind of the powerful urban planner Robert Moses, who felt the new stadium should be built in Queens. As a result, the Dodgers moved to Los Angeles following the 1957 season.

Although there may have been no place in baseball as sentimental as Ebbets, others were similarly endearing to their fans. The Polo Grounds, home of the New York Giants, was another of the old ballparks that was so special. But the Giants were having problems of their own, having suffered through three straight poor seasons since their 1954 championship.

The Polo Grounds stadium was falling apart, and attendance was down. Giants majority owner Horace Stoneham considered a move to Minneapolis-St. Paul, the home of his club's highest-classification minor league team, and then pursued San Francisco.

Both New York stadiums been tucked into what space was available amid buildings and businesses. The same was true of Crosley Field in Cincinnati. That is the way baseball stadiums were built back then.

It was the reason the parks were not symmetrical in the least as the dimensions were dictated by the size and layout of available property. The fact that stadiums were built to fit the space made for some very short distances from home plate to outfield fences, and in some cases, some very long distances, as well as numerous quirks that gave those old ballparks their identity.

As a result, outfield walls had lots of bends, crooks, nooks, and crannies. Visiting teams' outfielders frequently looked lost as they tried to play caroms that took unexpected bounces off the walls. It all made for character. The old baseball parks had a lot of character.

Just two of those old tabernacles remain—Wrigley Field, home of the Chicago Cubs, and Fenway Park, home of the Boston Red Sox. Wrigley was built in 1914 and became the Cubs' home two years later. Fenway opened in 1912.

Yankee Stadium was built in 1923, but has been replaced by a new home of the same name, located right across the street in the Bronx from the old ballpark.

The Dodgers enjoyed a long and glorious run in Brooklyn. They moved into brand-new Ebbets Field at the start of the 1913 season. Built where a garbage dump was once located, the storied park cost $750,000 to construct.

In the 45 years that Ebbets was their home, the Dodgers won nine National League pennants and one World Series championship, defeating the dreaded Yankees in 1955.

The right-field wall at Ebbets Field was 38 feet high, with a screen at the top half and concrete on the bottom half. The concrete part angled in toward the warning track and the huge scoreboard jutted out five feet from the wall at an angle of 45 degrees.

It has been estimated that balls could come off that wall at nearly 300 different angles, and Dodgers right fielder Carl Furillo knew them all and played them all like a master. The second deck overhung into center field.

Ebbets Field was loaded with personality. It had a rotunda enclosed in marble, and the floor had tiles that represented the stitches on a baseball. There was also a chandelier with 12 baseball bat arms holding 12 globes shaped like baseballs.

In right-center field, there was a metal gate with a gap that allowed youngsters a chance to watch games. The center of the domed ceiling was twenty-seven feet high.

By the mid-1950s, Ebbets Field had become outdated. It was in need of extensive repair, had a small seating capacity of 32,000, and there was almost no parking around the stadium.

Real estate developer Marvin Kratter purchased Ebbets Field in October of 1956. Part of the deal provided Dodgers owner Walter O'Malley with a three-year lease to keep the Dodgers in the stadium.

The following January, Kratter gave O'Malley two more years on his lease, meaning the Dodgers could have remained in Ebbets Field until 1961.

When O'Malley could not acquire the land he desired to build a new stadium, he moved the club to the West Coast following the 1957 season. In 1958, the team became the Los Angeles Dodgers.

After the Dodgers left Brooklyn, there was no use for the old ballpark, still filled with nostalgia, but lacking a major league team and fans. Ebbets Field was gone but not forgotten, fans' tales swelling in Bunyanesque fashion. The old ball yard has been embellished with time, its memory providing a romantic look back at the good old days.

In truth, the ballpark had become antiquated, a less than attractive place to watch a big league baseball game. It was dingy, drab, and dirty.

The Dodgers and their fans might have been major league, but the place they were playing was not.

The demolition of Ebbets Field began February 23, 1960. The lights and the scoreboard from the stadium were bought and used by minor league teams. There are apartments where the stadium once stood. A plaque is all that remains as a reminder of Ebbets Field.

The Polo Grounds closed down for big league baseball after the Giants left New York for San Francisco following the 1957 season.

The sun never shone more brightly at the Polo Grounds
than when Willie Mays was there.

But the old ballpark that stood between Coogan's Bluff and the Harlem River was given a new life in 1962 when the expansion New York Mets took up residence. They stayed just two years before moving into Shea Stadium for the 1964 season.

The site of Bobby Thomson's fairy tale home run that gave the Giants the 1951 National League pennant and Willie Mays' over-the-shoulder catch of Vic Wertz's drive in the 1954 World Series, the Polo Grounds were demolished in 1964.

Ironically, the same wrecking ball used to level Ebbets Field was swinging in the Polo Grounds when the sad event began April 10.

Crosley Field was the home of the Cincinnati Reds from 1912 through June 24, 1970. It was the first major league park with lights for playing night games and was among the smallest parks in the majors, both in seating capacity and size of the field.

The Terrace was the most famous, or infamous, feature of Crosley Field. Many of the older ballparks had a terrace, which compensated for the difference between field level and street level on a sloping piece of land.

The slope at Crosley was trouble for a lot of outfielders, most of them from visiting teams because they were not familiar with it. Babe Ruth suffered as much embarrassment as anybody. Playing for the Boston Braves in his last season, 1935, the Babe was running up The Terrace and fell on his face.

Frank Robinson, who played left field much of his 10 years with the Reds, loved The Terrace. So much that, when Baltimore was planning its new Camden Yards ballpark, Robinson, then an Orioles executive, tried to get the club to put a terrace in left field.

The Reds' last game at Crosley Field was June 24, 1970. During closing ceremonies for the ballpark, home plate was taken out of the ground and transported by helicopter to Riverfront Stadium, where it was installed.

The city of Cincinnati used Crosley as a vehicle impound lot for two years before demolishing it in the summer of 1972.

There was a rage during the 1960s over "cookie cutter ballparks." All of them were similar and symmetrical, and all were built with the idea of saving money, or at least, getting the absolute most for the investment.

That was because they were planned to be used for major league baseball games and National Football League games. Blueprints were drawn during the decade for eight of these stadiums, which, when completed, looked very much alike.

A look at the eight ballparks' dimensions demonstrates why the term "cookie cutter" was appropriate:

Robert F. Kennedy Stadium (Washington, D.C.)—right- and left-field lines, 335 feet, center field, 408; Shea Stadium (New York)—right and left, 330 feet, center, 410; Fulton-County Stadium (Atlanta)—right and left, 325, center, 402; Busch Stadium (St. Louis)—right- and left-field lines, 330, center, 414; Jack Murphy Stadium (San Diego)—right and left—330, center, 420; Riverfront Stadium (Cincinnati)—right and left, 325, center, 393; Three Rivers Stadium (Pittsburgh)—right and left, 340, center, 410; and Veterans Stadium (Philadelphia)—right and left, 330, center, 408.

The first of the eight to open was Robert F. Kennedy (RFK) Stadium in Washington as the expansion Senators had a new stadium in 1962, their second season. RFK actually opened right after the Senators' inaugural 1961 season and was ready for the Redskins' NFL campaign that year.

Shea Stadium was the Mets' home, beginning in 1964.

Fulton County Stadium was ready for the Braves in 1965, but the team was not allowed to move until the next year. So the Atlanta Crackers of the International League were the first team to use the new ballpark. Then, in 1966, the Braves moved from Milwaukee, and the NFL expansion Falcons played their first season.

The St. Louis Cardinals vacated old Busch Stadium (formerly Sportsman's Park) after the 1965 season. The football Cardinals and the baseball Cardinals moved into the second of three Busch ballparks in 1966.

Jack Murphy Stadium, originally called San Diego Stadium, was completed in 1967. It became the home of the San Diego Padres when they were added as a major league expansion team in 1969. The name changed to Qualcomm Stadium in 1997.

Riverfront Stadium opened for the Cincinnati Reds in June of 1970. The name was changed to Cinergy Field in 1996.

Three Rivers Stadium became the home of the Pittsburgh Pirates on July 16, 1970. In 1971, it hosted the first World Series game played at night as the Pirates took on the Baltimore Orioles. "The House That Clemente Built" was named for its location at the junction of the Allegheny River and Monongahela River, which forms the Ohio River.

The Philadelphia Phillies began the 1971 season in Veterans Stadium. It was named by the Philadelphia City Council in honor of the veterans of all wars.

Chapter 14

1966: Pulling an Ace Out of the Hat

March 6, 1961, may have been the day of the New York Mets' birth. But the day they got life was April 3, 1966.

That is when the Mets' name was pulled out of a hat in what amounted to a three-team lottery for the services of pitching prospect Tom Seaver.

Seaver, who pitched for the University of Southern Cal, was picked by the Los Angeles Dodgers in the 1965 draft. Seaver asked for a $70,000 bonus and the Dodgers refused. So he did not sign.

Seaver, a Californian who had grown up a fan of Henry Aaron, Eddie Mathews, **Joe Adcock**, and the rest of the Milwaukee Braves, was then drafted by the Braves in January of 1966 and signed with them one month later.

Major League Baseball Commissioner William Eckert termed the contract void on March 2. His reason was that Southern Cal had played two exhibition games against professional teams, though Seaver did not play in either.

Seaver then planned to finish out his college baseball season, but the NCAA said he was ineligible, ruling that his signing a contract with the Braves took away his amateur status.

Eckert said other major league teams could have the chance to match the Braves' offer of $51,000. The Cleveland Indians, New York Mets, and Philadelphia Phillies did that. The three names were put in a hat, and the Mets' name was drawn.

Pitching for New York's Triple-A team in Jacksonville, Seaver worked 210 innings and 10 complete games. His record was 12–12, with a 3.13 earned run average and 188 strikeouts.

Eventually called Tom Terrific and The Franchise, the right-hander was the pillar of the Mets' rotation the next year.

AS FOR THE BRAVES, they were in a new home for the 1966 season, having headed South to Atlanta after spending 14 years in Milwaukee. The Braves moved from Boston to Milwaukee after the 1951 season, and they received an enthusiastic welcome. Their first season in County Stadium was a huge success in every way. The '52 Braves finished 30 games over .500 and drew 1.8 million customers, a National League record at that time.

Turnstiles continued to whirl in Milwaukee, attendance hitting a high of more than two million in 1957 when the Braves beat the Yankees in the World Series.

A gradual decline in attendance followed, resulting in the sale of the Braves in 1962 and their eventual new Atlanta home in 1966. The club's first season in the South produced a fifth-place finish in the National League and total attendance over a million and a half.

The Braves played their first game in Atlanta April 12, 1966, losing to the Pittsburgh Pirates, 3–2, on a Willie Stargell two-run home run. It came in the 13th inning off **Tony Cloninger**, who pitched a complete game.

Joe Torre hit the first home run in Atlanta Stadium in the fifth inning. He homered again in the 13th. The attendance for the night game was 50,671.

THE ORIOLES ALSO MADE a big move in 1966. Into first place and on to a World Series championship.

Bogged in the second-division swamps of the American League throughout the 1950s, Baltimore began the new decade by vaulting to second place even if it was eight games behind the Yankees.

The Orioles finished no better than third the next five years before receiving three potent injections. The first came from Frank Robinson, who went to Baltimore in The Bad Trade; the second was a second wave of young arms; and the third was a deep bullpen.

Robinson, who had been the National League Most Valuable Player in 1961 when he was with Cincinnati, proceeded to win the American League MVP award as well as the triple crown in 1966, his first year with the Orioles.

Wave One consisted of Chuck Estrada, Jack Fisher, Milt Pappas, and Steve Barber. That quartet lifted the Orioles into the first division in the early '60s.

Wave Two was comprised of Dave McNally, Jim Palmer, Wally Bunker, and holdover Barber. The foursome, all 28 and younger, each was a double-figure winner in '66.

As for that bullpen, **Stu Miller, Eddie Fisher, Moe Drabowsky, Eddie Watt,** and **Dick Hall** combined for 35 wins and 49 saves. Slowballers Miller and Fisher led the way, while Drabowsky provided lots of laughs, 96 innings out of the pen, and a 6–0 record.

Miller, whose changeup was his fastball, relieved 51 times, winning nine games and saving 18 others with a 2.25 earned run average. Fisher, who relied mainly on a knuckleball, earned 14 saves with a 2.64 after coming over in a June trade with the White Sox.

Watt, a rookie, topped the five right-handers with 145 innings, the number boosted by 13 starts made when Barber was on the shelf. Watt did not start again in his nine remaining years in baseball.

Frank Robinson led the American League with 49 home runs, 122 RBIs, and a .316 batting average, as well as runs scored with 122. Brooks Robinson added 23 homers and 100 RBIs, with Boog Powell hitting 34 long balls and knocking in 109.

The Birds also committed the fewest errors in the league. They were strong up the middle with Gold Glover **Luis Aparicio** at short, second baseman **Davey Johnson,** and center fielder **Paul Blair** both eventual Gold Glove winners.

Aparicio, who was voted into Cooperstown, was also a great baserunner and fielder stealing more than 50 bases four times and collecting 9 Gold Gloves, provided an extremely steadying influence in Baltimore just as he had in Chicago.

In 1959, Little Louie had injected most of the go into the Go-Go White Sox who won the American League pennant. He swiped 56 bases and finished second in the MVP voting behind double-play buddy Nellie Fox.

Traded to the Orioles before the 1963 season, a 32-year-old Aparicio played a sparkling shortstop while igniting the offense from his leadoff spot with 182 hits and 97 runs.

No wonder manager Hank Bauer did not experience September stress. Baltimore won 97 times and took the AL by nine games.

Luis Aparicio led the American League in steals his first 9 years in the league, helping to revive stolen bases as a major weapon in baseball. (National Baseball Hall of Fame and Museum)

MOE DRABOWSKY MAY NOT have been the MVP of the 1966 World Series, but he was certainly The Catalyst.

Baseball was always a kid's game for the big right-hander, a native of Poland who was signed as a bonus baby by the Chicago Cubs. At 21 years of age, he joined Dick Drott, 20, in 1957 to give the Cubbies a promising one-two pitching punch.

Drabowsky won 13 games and Drott 15 that season, but neither ever hit the double-figure win column for Chicago again. After going 14–21 over the next two years, Drabowsky spent much of 1960 and '61 in the minor leagues.

He was traded to Milwaukee during spring training in 1961 and was the property of five major league teams in five years after leaving Chicago.

Drabowsky landed in Baltimore in November of 1965, when the Orioles took him in the rule 5 from the Cardinals (for whom he never played.) His career was rejuvenated under manager Hank Bauer and pitching coach Harry Brecheen.

In 1966, Drabowsky appeared in 41 games with the Orioles, 38 in relief. He finished with a 6–0 record, six saves, 2.81 ERA, and 98 strikeouts in 96 innings, issuing just 2.7 walks per nine innings.

Game One of the World Series, played in Los Angeles, provided the stage for the performance of his career. Left-hander Dave McNally was the Orioles' starter. Right-hander Don Drysdale was on the mound for the Dodgers.

Baltimore got to Drysdale right away. Frank Robinson and Brooks Robinson went deep back-to-back in the first inning, Frank smacking a two-run homer and Brooks following with another long ball.

The Orioles added a run in the second and Jim Lefebvre homered for L.A. in the same inning. Baltimore was up, 4–1, when McNally suddenly lost his control in the bottom of the third.

After one out, he walked Lou Johnson, Tommy Davis, and Lefebvre. Drabowsky was summoned from the bullpen, and he struck out Wes Parker. He walked Jim Gilliam to force in a run, then got John Roseboro on a foul out to the catcher.

Drabowsky then proceeded to strike out the side in the fourth and fifth innings. He fanned six Dodgers in a row, got L.A. three up and three down in the sixth and added a K to start the seventh. Eleven straight batters he had set down.

With one out, Maury Wills drew a walk and Willie Davis singled. And that was it. Drabowsky retired the last eight Dodgers he faced, allowing one hit over six and two-thirds innings, while striking out eleven. Eleven whiffs in relief. A World Series record that still stands.

The Orioles won, 5–2, and the stunned Dodgers never recovered. They did not score another run in the Series. Jim Palmer shut them out. So did Wally Bunker. So did McNally.

Ignited by Drabowsky, Baltimore pitchers did not give up a run over the last 33 and two-thirds innings in sweeping the World Series.

He was one of those guys who really enjoyed the game. He had fun and was known for his pranks as much as his pitching. He once gave the commissioner of baseball a hot foot, called in a take-out order to a Hong Kong restaurant from the bullpen phone, and put goldfish in a water cooler.

Drabowsky pitched in 88 games, all in relief, over the next two seasons with the Orioles, winning 11 and saving 19, while compiling ERAs of 1.60 and 1.91.

The 1972 season was his last in baseball. In 17 years, he pitched for seven teams, two of them twice, and had a lot of laughs doing it.

NEGRO LEAGUE STARS such as **Josh Gibson, Buck Leonard,** Buck O'Neil, and **James "Cool Papa" Bell** never had a chance to play at all in the majors.

One of the most popular and eternal "what if" baseball discussions wonders just how illustrious their careers might have been had they been spent in the big leagues. Ted Williams shared such feelings during his 1966 induction to the Baseball Hall of Fame.

His speech included the following words: "I have been a very lucky guy to have worn a baseball uniform, and I hope some day the names of Satchel Paige and Josh Gibson in some way can be added as a symbol of the great Negro players who are not here only because they weren't given a chance."

Williams, who was often profane, was profound that day at Cooperstown. The Hall of Fame, in large part in reaction to Williams' speech, has recognized 35 Negro Leaguers.

The Negro Leagues produced 57 major league players. Heading the list are Hall of Fame members Aaron, Banks, Campanella, Doby, **Monte Irvin**, Mays, Paige, and Jackie Robinson.

STARTING IN 1966—Steve Carlton, Davey Johnson, Tommie Agee, Ferguson Jenkins, George Scott, Don Sutton, Tommy Helms, Tito Fuentes, Jim Nash, Blue Moon Odom, Randy Hundley, Roy White, Art Shamsky.

Rookies of the Year were Agee and Helms.

Scott, the Boomer, smacked 27 home runs with 90 RBIs and showed nice defensive skills at first base. Nash went 12–1 with a 2.06, then won 56 more games over the last six years of his career. Hundley, a catcher whose son Todd caught in the majors, hit 19 homers and never matched that total in 13 more seasons though he was a true workhorse behind the plate and a National League All Star X times.

Sutton jumped into the Los Angeles Dodgers' starting rotation with Sandy Koufax and Don Drysdale as a 21-year-old rookie and stayed there 15 years. The right-hander made 31 or more starts 14 of those seasons.

He was a double-figure winner 21 of his 23 big league seasons, finishing with 324 victories, 5,282 innings pitched, and 3,574 strikeouts to earn a plaque in Cooperstown. Sutton wasn't just consistent; he was consistently outstanding.

Johnson played on a World Series champion with Baltimore as a rookie, won three Gold Gloves, and was a four-time All-Star. He hit 136 career home runs, 43 with the 1973 Atlanta Braves. He managed 17 years and won a World Series with the Mets.

Agee smashed 22 home runs and stole a career-high 44 bases for the White Sox as a rookie. In 1969–70, he hit 50 homers and drove in 151 runs for the Mets.

Helms batted .284 as the Reds' third baseman in 1966. He later won two Gold Gloves as Cincinnati's second baseman.

ENDING IN 1966—Sandy Koufax, Joe Adcock, Joey Jay, Frank Malzone, Harvey Kuenn, Roger Craig, **Don Blasingame, Eddie Kasko,** Jim Gilliam, **Roy McMillan,** Robin Roberts, **Del Crandall, Wes Covington, Joe Nuxhall.**

Nuxhall had two careers with the Cincinnati Reds. The southpaw pitcher arrived in the majors at the age of 15, getting battered in two-thirds of an inning, the youngest player to ever appear in a big league game. He did not take the mound in the big leagues again until eight years later and won 64 games for the Reds in a five-year span.

After bouncing around with a couple of other teams with not-so-strong results, Nuxhall returned to the Reds in his early 30s and won 46 games over the last five years, ending up a strong 135–117 for his career.

Kuenn was more recently known for the Harvey's Wallbangers teams he managed in Milwaukee, taking the Brewers to their lone World Series. The 1953 American League Rookie of the Year, playing for the Detroit Tiger, he enjoyed a notable playing career as well.

Kuenn batted over .300 eight times, including 1959 when he led the AL with a .353 average. At 22, he led the league in hits with 209 for the first of four occasions, and followed that up in 1954 with 201, in a campaign in which, amazingly, Kuenn fanned only 13 times in nearly 700 plate appearances. Kuenn, a .303 lifetime hitter, was an All-Star eight straight years, and was famously traded straight up for slugger Rocky Colavito.

Roberts was The Workhorse. He made at least 40 starts seven times and pitched 300-plus innings six straight seasons, winning 20 or more in each of them. He won 28 games in 1952, 23 all of the next three years.

The right-hander earned membership into the Hall of Fame with 286 victories and 4,688 innings pitched over 19 seasons.

Adcock was a power-hitting first baseman who hit 239 home runs in 10 years with the Milwaukee Braves. Four came in one game at Ebbets Field in 1954. In his fifth at-bat that day, he doubled off the top of the wall. He clouted 38 homers in 1956 and 35 in '61, driving in over 100 runs both years.

In 1953, Adcock became the first player to hit a ball over the Polo Grounds center field fence. Hank Aaron and Lou Brock are the only others to do it.

LAST PITCH OF 1966 SEASON—Orioles Dave McNally to LA's Lou Johnson. The Dodgers' right fielder flied out to center fielder Paul Blair, giving Baltimore a 1–0 win in Memorial Stadium. McNally's four-hitter in Game Four capped the Orioles' World Series sweep.

Chapter 15

A Talk with Tom Terrific

(AUTHOR'S NOTE: This interview is from a 2008 telephone interview, conducted during my research for this book. The Hall of Famer, who lived in California at the time—and still does—graciously agreed to speak with me and share some of his pitching wisdom. We spoke for more than and hour and he was so articulate and insightful about the art of pitching, I knew the only way to do justice to the material would be to reproduce the entirely of what he said.)

It was not at all disappointing to be picked by the Mets. All I saw was that it was a start to whatever it was going to be, a beginning of an unknown phase of my life. This individual has a chance to play major league baseball. You never know before that happens.

I was a late bloomer. When I was a junior in high school, I played junior varsity baseball. But what happens is, you go, "I have a chance to play professional baseball," and you think that is something that happens to other people.

Then, all of a sudden, I went right to Triple A. But I was 21 and had been in the marine corps, and I had two and a half years of college under my belt.

Control was the one part of the puzzle where I was very fortuitous, in the sense that when I was younger, I was not a hard thrower. I had to pitch to get people out. Not throw. Pitch. The learning curve of pitching, which really never ends, started at a young age for me.

I was always adjusting, always learning. Experiences, not just experience, made me better.

Was I intimidated by facing Aaron, Clemente, and those kinds of hitters? I don't think I was intimidated. It's a matter of semantics or choice of words. But being, in some cases, in awe. Your childhood dreams and your adult dreams become a reality.

Actually, that did not last very long for me. That kind of thinking. I pitched against Aaron in Atlanta for the first time, and I knew his every physical move—how he put the bat at his belt and put his helmet on, and I couldn't watch him.

Because I was disciplined enough to know what my job was, so I turned away till he got in the box. I was trying to control my emotions to not let the awe, the hero worship, dominate me. Not let that part of your brain take over.

The first time I faced Aaron, I ran my sinker in right below the belt buckle, and he hit a ground ball to shortstop. And I'm thinking, "I just got Henry Aaron out." Hard to keep from showing emotion, but you can't do that.

Then, the second time we went around the lineup, Henry came up again. And I threw that same kind of pitch, and I got it right where I wanted it. Only, he didn't stride the same way. He opened up his stride, looked for that pitch inside, and hit a home run down the left-field line. He made an adjustment.

If there is one lesson that I learned that is most important, that is it right there. I said, "Oh, that's why these guys are good." You know, in a sense, it was "Thank you, Henry Aaron."

Now, that's why these guys excel, and excel at a very high level for a long period of time. They can think and adjust. And we all have the physical ability to do that.

The lesson in those two at-bats ratcheted me up 10 notches. The lesson learned was worth the home run. That was 1967, and I can still see it. It was so important in the education process. The important part, the genesis of what I'm talking about is that those players who continue to do well learn from those lessons.

It doesn't take three times or five times. In one little at-bat, there can be a lesson that lasts a lifetime, a career.

I learn from experience. I don't think there's any doubt that had a lot to do with 311 (wins). I had the education of pitching in the big leagues and what it takes to do that for a long period of time.

Was there anything special about the '60s? A lot of it is emotional . . . certain (of those "awe") players that added an emotional aspect for young guys who got to play against them in that time frame.

The Mays, Aarons, McCoveys, Clementes, the Richie Allens, Stargells, Gibson, Fergie Jenkins . . . the top-drawer professionals, those kinds of people.

I've thought that maybe players were better back in the '60s, but I think that's probably generational and emotional, good-old-days stuff. We all like to think they were better in our day. But Derek Jeter could play any time. So could Tony Gwynn.

I would say, arguably, that you've got Aaron, Mays, and Mantle all in the same era, and you're not going to find three more like them. Any time. You could say the same thing about Ted Williams, Stan Musial, and Bob Feller.

Tom Seaver combined perfect mechanics with great mound savvy to become one of the greatest starting pitchers in major league history. (National Baseball Hall of Fame and Museum).

Now, as for today's starting pitchers and the way they're doing things. More to the point, the way they are made to do things. I think it's more financial than anything else.

They put so much money into these guys, these arms, and they don't want them to get hurt. So they protect them. Over-protect them. Throwing is good for a pitcher. Cut down on his throwing, and he hurts his arm easier. It's not the other way around.

So, they protect these young guys . . . sometimes the word pamper is used, sometimes it's the right word. And they still get hurt. Often. Tommy John surgeries all over the place.

You arbitrarily pick a number . . . this guy, you don't want him throwing over 100 pitches in a game. All the starting pitcher knows, is thinking about, is 100 pitches. He is programmed that way.

Well, everybody has a pitch count. I had a pitch count. When I pitched, I had a pitch count; there's no question about it. And my max was about 135. The thing is, I knew that was where I was.

And the last three innings, I would know—ballpark, anyway— how many pitches I had left. It would usually take me to the eighth or ninth inning.

You're out there, and you know you got around this many pitches left. And the number eight hitter comes up there. You don't spend eight pitches to get him out. You throw three pitches, and he hits a ground ball to the shortstop.

Don't waste them on number eight, because other times, you're going to need some pitches to work with. You get Billy Williams up there and you've got runners on first and third. You are going to need some pitches to work with. That's where you spend them.

We're not all the same. I don't go along with having a set number for everybody across the board. I would say Koosman (Jerry) could probably throw 145 pitches and Nolan (Ryan) could throw 150 or 155. Nolan could throw forever.

What they do today is look for a reason to take pitchers out. You're out there on the mound, thinking, "Well, am I going to get taken out of this thing?" Or, "do I not pitch to this guy because I know they're going to come take me out?"

All this stuff you conjure up, and you start expecting to come out. Looking for someone to come and get you.

Back then, if you looked to the dugout, they turned away. They expected me—and all the starters—to get out of the jam. We were expected to.

That's a learning curve, too. Well, you can look at it two ways. You've struggled, and it's the seventh inning, and you look over, and there's nobody (warming up) in the bullpen. Gil Hodges and Rube Walker are looking at you, and what are they saying?

That you are good enough to get out of this. You're good enough. You don't need help. You're not getting any help. Hey, great! Go get 'em!

You make a couple of bad pitches, and you get yourself a bad situation. And runners are here and there, and the pitching coach or the manager comes to the mound, and he says, "You're okay."

You take a breath and go back to zero. Go back to the ABCs of pitching. That coach or manager says you will get out of this. You're throwing well. He pats you on the back and goes back to the dugout.

They'd sit down and watch, and they made you believe that you could do it. That you would do it. Expectations. The ones they (the managers and coaches) had for you. And, as a result, the ones you had for yourself. You also believed you would do it.

The ABCs of pitching. There is always a gray area there. But for me, the first pitch to every hitter who walks up there is going to be a strike. Because, then you can get them out on two pitches. And you're going to throw four pitches if you are going to walk him.

Okay, that's A—start with a strike. B, the first guy who walks up there is going to be an out. The first out in the inning. You've got to think that way. You've got to pitch that way. You can't mess around, let the leadoff hitter get on base, and start digging yourself a hole.

Basically, that's the fundamental foundation. The building blocks of pitching. Excellence. That's what you're after. You pitch for excellence. It requires a plan.

You've got to get ahead of that first guy who comes up there, and that first guy is an out.

C, the last thing . . . that guy hitting eighth, he goes oh for four. You let number eight get on base, and he's saying, "Thank you very much."

You don't do that. Can't do that.

For me, it was, "Thou shalt not dig myself a hole."

You know, if you tell a pitcher he can only throw this many pitches, that he's coming out after this number, then that's what he's going to believe.

He isn't bearing down and thinking, "I'm going nine." No, he gets to a point, and he's thinking, "They're going to come and get me." Expectations.

Quality start? What's that? For me—for every starting pitcher back then—that meant nine innings and a win. There was no name for it. That was expected. By the managers and pitching coaches. By the pitchers themselves.

No one went out there to pitch six innings. We went out there for nine. They played nine. We were thinking we'd pitch nine.

Chapter 16

1967: The Summer of Yaz

Carl Yastrzemski had a boulder on his shoulders in the spring of 1961. He was facing the same hurdles that await any rookie, plus, he was staring into the intimidating shadow of Ted Williams.

The Splendid Splinter had retired the year before, leaving a vacancy and a legacy in left field with the Boston Red Sox. Inevitably, the new left fielder would be compared to Williams.

The son of a Long Island potato farmer, Yaz had wanted to play for the New York Yankees, but they would not meet his dad's $100,000 demand. Ultimately, he signed with Boston for $108,000, a two-year $10,000 Triple-A contract, and college tuition.

In 1959, his first year in pro baseball, Yastrzemski batted a league-leading .377 for the Class-B Raleigh Caps and was named Carolina League MVP despite scuffling defensively while playing shortstop and second base.

The next season, at Triple-A Minneapolis, he was switched to left field. He only hit seven home runs, though, and there were questions about his ability to hit for power.

The big concern was that most of Yaz's power was to the opposite field. Even though that made the Green Monster friendly for the young left-handed hitter, it did not forecast big home run numbers. As a Red Sox rookie, his first four homers were to left, and he hit just 11 home runs that season.

Yastrzemski said Williams' hitting theories were too confusing for him. Yaz eventually learned to pull the ball, and he hit 40 or more home runs three times in a span of four seasons.

He won three batting titles and became the first American League player with at least 400 homers and 3,000 hits. He played 23 years in the majors, all with the Red Sox.

Yaz was the MVP in 1967, when he won the triple crown. One thing he did that Williams did not is to come through in the World Series, though he was battling an injury at the time. In the 1946 Series, Williams had five singles in 25 at-bats with one RBI.

Yastrzemski batted .352 with nine RBIs in 14 Series games, and he hit three home runs with a .400 average in the 1967 World Series.

Yaz was spectacular in '67, and it wasn't just his statistics; it was his ability to come through in big situations. Almost every time, especially during the final month of the season.

He led the American League in batting (.326), home runs (44, tied with Harmon Killebrew), RBIs (121), runs scored (112), hits (189), on-base percentage (.418), and slugging percentage (.622).

Yastrzemski also had a sterling defensive season, one of the best ever by a left fielder. Playing balls off Fenway Park's Green Monster like a kid plays tennis balls off his garage door at home, the seven-time Gold Glover made strong, accurate throws to nail 13 runners and prevent many more from taking another base.

The Red Sox entered September of 1967 in a four-horse race for the American League pennant. Boston led Minnesota by a half game, and was one and a half up on both Detroit and Chicago.

In that final nerve-wrenching month, Yaz hit .417, clouting nine homers and driving in 26 runs in 27 games. Over the last 13 games, he batted .500 with 18 RBIs.

Yastrzemski had plenty of pressure the entire summer as the Red Sox, in their drive for a title, relied heavily on him. That pressure increased on August 18 when **Tony Conigliaro** was hit in the face by a **Jack Hamilton** fastball.

The right fielder, who had already surpassed the 100-homer mark at the age of 22, had 20 home runs and 67 RBIs when he went down for the season. Not only did Boston lose Tony C's bat, they lost his protection of Yaz in the lineup.

With Yastrzemski batting third and Conigliaro fourth, pitchers could not afford to pitch around Yaz. That changed when there was no Tony C.

Yaz got seven hits in eight at-bats with six RBIs in the final two days. Over the final dozen games of the season, he batted .523 with five home runs, 16 runs driven in, and 14 runs scored.

Captain Carl was truly magnificent when the games counted most.

THE 1967 WORLD SERIES was incredible. Seven games, of course. Carl Yastrzemski hit three home runs. Bob Gibson pitched three complete-game victories and homered.

The Cardinals and Red Sox split in Boston; then the Cards took the next two. The Sox won Game Five in St. Louis to stay alive before evening things at home. Then Gibson sealed the whole deal and the MVP award with a three-hitter.

Bob Gibson started 9 World Series games in his career. He won 7, totaled 81 IP and 93 strikeouts, allowed just 55 hits and 17 walks, and had an ERA of 1.89. (National Baseball Hall of Fame and Museum).

Jim Lonborg threw a one-hitter and a three-hitter before getting bashed in Game 7. Roger Maris batted .348 and drove in a Series-high seven runs.

Lou Brock put on a show of his own with eight runs, 12 hits, a .414 batting average, and seven stolen bases—all highs for the Series.

Yaz continued what he had been doing since spring—hitting like crazy and producing in the clutch. He had 10 hits, five for extra bases, five RBIs, and a .400 average.

PITCHING DOMINANCE WAS A PROMINENT theme of the 1960s, and Bob Gibson is synonymous with that. His 1968 season of brilliance and his mastery in three World Series place him on a pedestal, a mountain top even.

There is one more Gibson accomplishment that has to be included. Not so much an accomplishment, though, as it is a definition. Of his character, his unmatched determination, his toughness.

It was July 15, 1967, a Saturday at Busch Stadium in St. Louis. The Cardinals were up on the Pirates, 1–0, with Roberto Clemente leading off in the top of the fourth inning. Clemente smashed a line drive off the right leg of Gibson, reaching on an infield single.

The Cardinals' trainer went out, sprayed Gibson's leg with something, and put some tape above the ankle where the ball had struck the pitcher. To the surprise of no one, Gibson stayed in the game.

He walked Willie Stargell, retired Bill Mazeroski on a routine fly to center, then walked Donn Clendenon on a three-two pitch to load the bases. Gibson collapsed on the last pitch to Clendenon. A bone, already weakened by Clemente's shot, had snapped.

It was the fibula. Doctors projected that Gibson would miss six to eight weeks. After losing that game, the Cardinals were 51–34 and owned a four-game lead over the rest of the National League. Gibson's record was 10–6 with a 3.52 earned run average.

Three youngsters picked up the slack in the Cardinal ace's absence. Nelson Briles, **Dick Hughes**, and Steve Carlton combined for 19 wins while Gibson was healing. Hughes, 29, and Carlton, 22, were in their first full big league seasons, and 23-year-old Briles was in his second.

Hughes, whose career ended the following year, went 16–6 with a 2.67 ERA. Carlton, the left-hander bound for the Hall of Fame, was 14–9 with a 2.98. Briles was 14–5 with a 2.43 and six saves as he came out of the bullpen 35 times to go with 14 starts.

Gibson returned September 7, with St. Louis holding a comfortable lead of 11 and a half games. After being out 54 days, he pitched five innings and allowed two runs in earning his 11th win. Five days later, he combined with Larry Jaster on a five-hit shutout of the Phillies.

Then came a complete-game three-hitter at Philadelphia. Gibson's third straight victory since his return was his 13th of the season. He was working himself in Fall Classic shape.

He worked eight innings and struck out 10 in a 2–1 loss to the Braves. Gibson's final tuneup was September 29 as he threw nine innings and allowed an unearned run, lowering his ERA under 3.00 for the season. That gave him four days rest before the World Series, also known as the Bob Gibson Special, opened in Boston.

NOT MANY PITCHERS GET BETTER with age, but it can be argued that Jim Bunning is one who did. Bunning went 17-15 in 1967, his age-35 season, with a sparkling ERA of 2.29, in 302.1 innings pitched! He also lead the league in strikeouts and shutouts, and finished second to Mike McCormick (22-10) in the Cy Young Award voting.

That Bunning pitched in eight All-Star games and zero post-season games speaks volumes about his big league career. In 18 innings pitched in the All-Star game, Bunning's ERA was a sparkling 1.00. Bunning spent 17 years in the majors, 15 as a regular starting pitcher who seldom missed a turn. The teams on which he played finished higher than fourth place only twice and never won a pennant.

He won 224 games and likely would have won quite a few more with more runs and better defense behind him. A 3.27 earned run average in 3,760 innings suggests as much.

Bunning was a 20-game winner for Detroit in 1957, his first full season in the rotation. Although he didn't hit the 20 mark again, he won 19 four times. He pitched two no-hitters, one a perfect game in 1964. He was the first pitcher since Cy Young to notch over 100 wins and 1,000 strikeouts in each league.

His first nine years were with the Tigers, who traded Bunning, then 32, to Philadelphia in December of 1963. In his first four seasons with the Phillies, he averaged 40 starts, 298 innings, 248 strikeouts, and 18.5 victories while throwing 23 shutouts with ERAs no higher than 2.63.

Known for knocking batters off the plate, he plunked 160 of them in his career and led the National League in that notorious category four years in a row.

ROD CAREW JOINED THE TWINS in 1967, and two years later, he led the American League in hitting. He and teammate Tony Oliva combined to win eight batting titles in a 10-year stretch, with Carew winning four in-a-row and six in a seven-year span.

Carew, who began as a second baseman, played first base the last half of his career. An excellent bunter with tremendous bat control, he won seven batting titles.

He missed the magical .400 mark by seven hits in 1977, when he hit .388 on the way to earning the American League MVP award. Carew was an All-Star his first 18 years, starting 15, and finished with 3,053 hits and a .328 average over 19 seasons.

He averaged nearly 19 stolen bases per year and swiped home 17 times.

REGGIE JACKSON NEVER MET a camera or headline that he didn't like. But, for all his show-boating, he was a likeable slugger who thrived in the spotlight.

He hit one home run in 118 at-bats in 1967, his first season in the big leagues. Jackson hit at least 23 homers the next 13 years and no fewer than 14 homers in each of his last 20 seasons.

Jackson hit 563 lifetime home runs, 18 more in the post season, including 10 in five World Series. His nickname of "Mr. October was well earned, for his play with the Yankees, and also for helping the A's to three consecutive World Series wins in the early 1970s. Jackson is the all-time whiff king with 2,597.

TONY PEREZ HOMERED OFF CATFISH HUNTER in the 15th inning to give the National League a 2–1 win in the 1967 All-Star Game held in Anaheim. Homers accounted for all of the runs, with Dick Allen and Brooks Robinson also connecting.

Continuing his phenomenal season, Carl Yastrzemski had two singles and a double. Tony Oliva and **Tim McCarver** each had a pair of hits. Perez was named MVP.

STARTING IN 1967 — Reggie Jackson, Cito Gaston, Joe Niekro, Tom Seaver, Gary Nolan, Reggie Smith, Mike Marshall, Dave Duncan, Mike Epstein, Rod Carew, Sparky Lyle, Rick Monday.

Seaver and Carew were Rookies of the Year.

Smith was a switch-hitter who hit for power and could run, a center- and right-fielder with a strong arm. He batted over .300 and combined for

47 home runs in 1969 and '70 for the Red Sox, his original team. He had 314 homers and 2,020 hits in 17 seasons.

Albert Walter Lyle pitched in 899 games over a 16-year major league career, and all of them were in relief. He finished 634 of those games, saving 238.

Traded to New York after four years with Boston, Lyle finished 56 of his 59 games and recorded 35 saves in his first season as a Yankee. He won the 1972 Cy Young with 13 wins, 26 saves, and a 2.17 ERA.

Nolan wasn't yet 19 when his major league career began. It ended before he turned 30. In between were tremendous success, pain, and disappointment.

The right-hander won 14 games for Cincinnati in 1967, then battled arm problems over the next 10 years. Nolan won 45 for the Reds from 1970–72 and had back-to-back 15-win seasons in '75–76. His lifetime record was 110–70, a .611 winning percentage.

Marshall defied traditional thought on rest needed by pitchers. The Doctor—he had a PhD in kinesiology, which is the study of body movement—operated almost daily. He pitched in 198 games in a two-year span with the Los Angeles Dodgers, 92 with 31 saves in 1973 and 106 with 15 wins, 21 saves, and a Cy Young Award the next season. He threw an all-time record 208 innings out of the bullpen in '74.

ENDING IN 1967—Don Larsen, **Jimmy Piersall**, Dick Groat, Whitey Ford, Smoky Burgess, **Lew Burdette**, Bob Buhl, George Altman, Curt Simmons, Moose Skowron, **Bob Uecker**, **Vernon Law**.

Burgess, tagged "Shake, Rattle and Roll" by Pirates broadcaster Bob Prince, could just plain hit. Any time. Any situation. His left-handed stance was so comfortable that he appeared to be sitting in a rocking chair with a bat in his hands.

Short and stocky, Burgess was a part-time catcher who eventually made pinch-hitting practically an art form. His ability to consistently get clutch hits and drive in key runs despite entering the game cold was uncanny. He had 145 lifetime pinch hits, 16 of them home runs. The six-time All-Star was a key member of Pittsburgh's 1960 World Series champion.

When you have teammates named Mantle, Berra, and Ford, it's easy to fade into the background. Such was the plight of Bill Skowron. But the Yankees' first baseman sure was appreciated by his teammates and manager.

The Moose came through often in the clutch and he hit for power, socking 165 home runs in nine years with the Yanks. He hit 23 or more homers four times and helped New York win four World Series titles. Traded to L.A., he then hit a home run to help the Dodgers beat the Pinstripes in the 1963 Series.

Larsen went 51–51 after his World Series perfect game. He worked out of the bullpen most of the late stages of a 14-year career and beat the Yankees for the Giants in a 1962 Series game. Larsen hit 14 big league home runs.

Piersall was a terrific center fielder who won two Gold Gloves and was selected to two All-Star Games. He enjoyed his reputation as a flake, proving it when he ran backwards around the bases upon hitting career home run No. 100.

Simmons won 17 games for the 1950 Whiz Kids, but was unable to pitch for the Phillies in the World Series because of military duty. That was the best season for the left-hander until 1964, when, at the age of 35, he won 18 for the World champion Cardinals.

LAST PITCH OF 1967 SEASON—Cardinals Bob Gibson to George Scott. Gibson blew strike three past the Red Sox first baseman, wrapping up a 7–2 Game Seven win in Boston and a World Series title.

Chapter 17

Clemente on Clemente

(AUTHOR'S NOTE: These words are directly from Roberto Clemente, from an in-person interview conducted August 1, 1970. I was in Atlanta to do stories on some Braves players for the Chattanooga Courier. I decided to also try to speak with Clemente, who was injured and not in Pittsburgh's lineup that day. The future Hall of Famer sat down at his locker and talked extensively prior to the game.)

Roberto Clemente won four batting titles. His rocket arm is still considered one of the best of all time, and he made sliding catches in the outfield long before they became trendy.

He had a reputation of being a complainer and somewhat of a hypochondriac, or being selfish and moody. There were whispers that he pouted when he was not named the league's Most Valuable Player after his Pittsburgh Pirates won the 1960 World Series.

In truth, Roberto Clemente was sad and often felt alone and misunderstood. He was a sensitive man whose feelings were hurt by a culture filled with prejudice. He did not begrudge teammate Dick Groat being named the '60 MVP; he just felt the season he had deserved more respect in the voting.

When he was hurt, writers made comments in columns suggesting Clemente could return to the lineup sooner or "play hurt" for the good of the team.

He was even mocked. Pittsburgh writers sometimes made fun of his use of the English language by writing words exactly as Clemente said them, making him look foolish in the process.

All of this gnawed at Clemente, tore his insides and made him feel unappreciated and ridiculed. In an interview at Atlanta's Fulton County Stadium in August of 1970, the Pirates' electrifying right fielder let his feelings out, sharing his frustrations and sadness.

Roberto Clemente's 166 career triples make him one of only
two batters (Musial with 177 is the other) who played in the 1960s or after to total
as many as 150. (National Baseball Hall of Fame and Museum).

He had been hit by a pitch from **Larry Dierker** of the Houston Astros six days earlier and had not been in the Pirates' lineup since. There was an encouraging sign, though, as Clemente had appeared in the previous night's game as a pinch-runner.

Game time for the Pirates meeting with the Braves was 3:10 on this Saturday afternoon. It was two hours before that, and a check of the Pittsburgh lineup posted in the locker room showed that Clemente again was not playing.

There was Clemente, standing in front of his cubicle. He wore his uniform pants, black stirrups with the gold rings, and a baseball undershirt—white with long black sleeves. His uniform shirt with number 21 on the back hung on the locker door.

The writer caught a break when he introduced himself as being from North Carolina, Clemente stuck out his right hand, smiled, and said, "Hey, I'm from Carolina also." (He was born in Carolina, Puerto Rico.) The ice was broken.

The writer explained that he wanted to talk to Clemente about his career and about how he had often been misunderstood by the media and, as a result, by fans.

He was a very proud and a very sensitive man. He was passionate about being one of the best baseball players of all time and about representing his country. He wanted to show the world what an outstanding person and athlete his home country had produced.

Much had been written and said about athletes, especially professional athletes, playing hurt, performing in spite of injuries because that is what they are paid to do. Athletes who sit out with ailments perceived by the press and public to be minor had often been maligned.

Clemente was one such athlete.

Anyone spending a few minutes in conversation with Roberto Clemente would realize that he was quite intelligent and articulate.

Learning a new language is never easy, especially when done on the fly. His first few years in the major leagues were also his first few years in the United States, and he was having to learn to speak English while being interviewed by people who wrote his words down for the public's digestion and inspection.

So, Roberto Clemente grabbed a nearby chair and invited me to sit down with him in front of his locker. Here is what he said:

"I feel I have been terribly misunderstood. I think many Latin ballplayers have been misunderstood. We are thought to be moody, very temperamental, and every time we voice an opinion or a feeling that does not go along with everybody else, that label of moody is thrown up at us. That is not fair.

"For me, though, it has been more than that. People—sports writers write it and then other people say it—criticize that I whine and complain about every little thing that bothers me, every little ache and pain.

"Let me say that I play baseball very hard ... as hard as anyone, harder than most. I give everything I've got—running after fly balls, making throws, hitting the baseball, and running the bases.

"Sometimes I crash into walls catching balls or trying to catch them. I have even had stitches as a result. To me, it is the only way to play; it is the only way to do anything.

"I do everything to the best of my ability. I don't loaf or take it easy, no matter what the score is, no matter where our team is in the standings.

"It is the only way I know. And it is a matter of pride. I don't ever want anyone to say that Roberto Clemente gave less than his best. But, really, that is what they are saying when they talk about me being a hypochondriac, making excuses for not playing.

"When I miss a game, it is because I am not physically able to give my best. If I try to play and cannot get to a fly ball, cannot run fast enough to a base, cannot swing the bat to hit the ball hard because something hurts, then that is not the true Roberto Clemente.

"To me, that would be hurting the team. And, also, I could get myself hurt worse and end up missing many more games. I think it is the smart thing to miss a game or a few and get better.

"Then the Pittsburgh Pirates will have the real Roberto Clemente back in the lineup. I think that is what the Pittsburgh Pirates and their fans would want.

"Listen, I do not like to miss baseball games. I love the game. I love to play it. I love showing that men from Puerto Rico can play baseball very, very well. Why would I want to miss a chance to do that?

"It's just that going out there and just halfway playing because my shoulder or my back hurts ... that would not be the whole Roberto Clemente. It would bother me deep down not to be able to get to a ball or hit a ball because something was hurting and to play poorly because of that.

"Don't you think that makes sense?"

The writer agreed that it made a lot of sense and added that there is no way one person can know how much another person is hurting.

"That is exactly right. That is what I have been telling the writers. They stand beside me and nod their heads, like they agree. Then they write in their newspapers that Roberto Clemente is a hypochondriac, that he looks for reasons to stay out of games. That makes me sad and it makes me angry. But what can I do?"

Whether intentional or not, writers had painted a picture of Clemente that was not at all accurate. He was depicted as looking for excuses not to play when, in fact, he wanted to play as much as he could and the best that he could.

Rising from his chair, Clemente pointed a finger and said, "There is one more thing I want to say, to clear up. I was never jealous of Dick Groat, and I never said I should have been the MVP instead of him."

The reference was to the 1960 voting for National League Most Valuable Player. Groat finished first, followed by teammate and third baseman Don Hoak. Clemente, who led the Pirates with 94 RBIs and batted .314, finished eighth on the ballot, right behind another teammate, pitcher Vernon Law.

"It just hurt me that I was not shown more respect for the season I had. I'm happy for my teammate and friend, Dick Groat. He is a great player and a great leader. I simply felt overlooked after having a very good season myself."

The Great One returned to the lineup a week later, getting a double and a home run and driving in two runs as the Pirates lost to the Mets. He finished the season with a .352 batting average.

After he was killed in a plane crash while trying to get supplies would get to earthquake-stricken Nicaragua, the Baseball Writers Association of America held a special election and waived the mandatory five-year waiting period for Clemente, voting him into the Hall of Fame.

He compiled a .317 lifetime batting average with 240 home runs, 1,305 RBI, and four batting titles and became the first Hispanic player inducted at Cooperstown.

Baseball Commissioner Bowie Kuhn said this in his eulogy to Clemente: "He gave the term 'complete' a new meaning. He made the word superstar seem inadequate. He had about him a touch of royalty."

Chapter 18

1968: Pitchers Rule

Bob Gibson was king in 1968. It was the Year of the Pitcher, and nobody was better. The St. Louis Cardinals right-hander wasn't just great; he was dominant. For the entire season.

Gibson was simply on another planet. He won 22 games, pitched 13 shutouts, completed 28 starts, and had a 1.12 earned run average, the lowest in the major leagues since 1914. His 304 innings pitched surpassed his hits allowed by more than 100.

The National League Cy Young winner and Most Valuable Player in '68, Gibson was a fabulous athlete. Overcoming health issues that included asthma, pneumonia, and a heart murmur, he received a basketball scholarship to Creighton University and once barnstormed with the Harlem Globetrotters.

"Bob Gibson threw everything hard," said Cubs outfielder George Altman. "He didn't throw that many off-speed pitches. You knew it was going to be a sinking fastball or a slider with him, but it didn't matter because he put the ball where he wanted it.

"He threw a heavy ball, too, so when you hit it, you didn't often hit it well. Sometimes it felt like he was knocking the bat out of your hands. And he didn't mind pitching inside."

Gibson was a fierce competitor who took everything personally. He didn't take kindly to a batter trying to bunt on him, and often he would later deck the guy who tried it. Same thing if a batter hit a home run off him.

"Mean" was a word used to describe Gibson. He didn't like hitters and didn't like being visited on the mound by his catcher, pitching coach, or manager. It was his mound when it was his day to pitch, and he didn't need anybody telling him what to do.

In 1968, Gibson was the poster pitcher for a year filled with outstanding mound performances. And much of the success—punctuated by astonishing numbers and deeds—was attributed in great part to two words that popped up frequently in the 1960s: Rule changes.

THE '60S WERE DISTINGUISHED by astounding mound feats, as pitching was the most definitive element of baseball in the decade. The pitching was not just very good; it was phenomenal.

Earned run averages were low, and so were batting averages. Thirty-four no-hitters were thrown during the decade, and pitchers set records that still have not been broken.

Twenty-one men who pitched in the 1960s wound up in the Hall of Fame. And while talent might seem explanation enough for such tremendous accomplishments, there was more to it than that.

The expanded strike zone, which became law in January of 1963, had an instant and definite impact. It was as much a detriment to the hitters as an advantage to the pitchers. It was like they had this weapon, and all of a sudden, it took on greater range and more power.

In 1968, the Year of the Pitcher, the major league collective earned run average plummeted to 2.98, and almost 21 percent of all games were shutouts. There were 21 pitchers with an ERA of 2.50 and lower.

Twenty teams combined to hit 1,995 home runs, just 891 in the National League, where the overall batting average was .243. The American League batted .230.

Carl Yastrzemski's .301 in 1968 is the lowest average ever to win a major league batting title, and he was one of only six players in the majors to hit .300 that season.

It was Yaz's third, and last, batting crown. **Danny Cater** of Oakland was second in the American League at .290. Pete Rose led National League at .335, followed by Pittsburgh's Matty Alou, .322; his brother, Felipe Alou, of Atlanta, .317; and Rose's Cincinnati teammate, **Alex Johnson**, .312. St. Louis' Curt Flood, No. 5 on the NL list, matched Yaz's .301 mark.

Roberto Clemente placed tenth in the National League batting race, his .291 marking the only time in his final 13 seasons that he failed to hit at least .312.

One of the crowning achievements of 1968 came from another pitcher who did not mind throwing inside. The Dodgers' Don Drysdale was an intimidating right-hander, especially tough on right-handed batters with his sidearm delivery that appeared to be coming from third base.

ON MAY 14, 1968, "BIG D" warmed up to pitch against the Chicago Cubs, having been victimized by anemic run support from his Dodger teammates.

His record was 1–3, with Los Angeles having scored a total of nine runs in his last eight starts. Drysdale threw a two-hitter at the Cubs that day and won, 1–0, starting a streak that would make history.

Drysdale then pitched another 1–0 gem, beating Houston. Next up were the Cardinals and Gibson, who allowed one hit over eight innings, but the Dodgers scratched out a 2–0 win.

Facing the Astros again, Drysdale got plenty of runs for a change. He had to escape two ninth-inning jams—two on and nobody out, and bases loaded and two outs—before winning, 5–0, to stretch his scoreless inning string to 36.

In his next start, Drysdale was leading the Giants, 3–0 after eight innings, in front of a large crowd at Dodger Stadium, when it appeared that the streak was in serious jeopardy.

Two walks and a single loaded the bases with nobody out, and when Drysdale plunked San Francisco catcher **Dick Dietz** on the arm with a fastball, it looked like the streak was over.

However, plate umpire Harry Wendelstedt ruled that Dietz had made no attempt to avoid being hit, and he called the pitch a ball, making the count 3–2. The Giants were livid, and an argument of nearly 10 minutes ensued.

When play resumed, Dietz flied to short right field, **Ty Cline** grounded into a force out at the plate, and **Jack Hyatt** popped out. That made five straight shutouts and 45 consecutive scoreless innings for Drysdale.

He pitched a record sixth shutout in a row and broke Carl Hubbell's National League record of 46 and a third scoreless innings when he three-hit the visiting Pirates, 5–0.

On June 8, with more than 50,000 in attendance at Dodger Stadium, Drysdale put up four more zeroes before the Phillies scored with two outs in the fifth.

His 58 and two-thirds scoreless innings broke **Walter Johnson's** major league record of 56. Drysdale continued to get few runs with which to work, finishing the season at 14–12 despite a 2.15 ERA.

A year later, Drysdale's career was over. A 5–4 record and shoulder trouble prompted him to retire from baseball in August of 1969 at the age of 33.

Denny McLain pitched a complete game win as a 19-year-old rookie in September of 1963, a game in which he also belted the only home run of his career. (National Baseball Hall of Fame and Museum)

DENNY McLAIN'S 1968 SEASON WAS HISTORIC. It just got lost to some degree in the afterglow of Gibson's six months of devastation.

McLain's 31–6 record made him the majors' first 30-game winner since **Dizzy Dean** (30–7) in 1934. Fifty years later, the feat still has not been accomplished again, nor is it likely to ever. The Detroit right-hander's earned run average in '68 was 1.96 over 336 innings, and he threw six shutouts, while fanning 280.

The guy was a character. Days after getting victory No. 30, he grooved a batting-practice fastball to Mickey Mantle to allow the Yankees star to smack one over the fence for his 535th home run, which put Mantle into sole possession of fourth place on the all-time home run list, passing Jimmie Foxx.

McLain, who threw a no-hitter in his first professional game, played the organ on The Ed Sullivan Show and made two albums. He owned and flew his own airplane and eventually got into a lot of trouble. There were connections to gambling and the mob, leading to a half-season suspension from baseball in 1970.

He was a 20-game winner in 1966 when he served up 42 home runs, and he followed his 31-win season with a 1969 performance that was also fantastic—24–9 with nine shutouts—which helped him earn back-to-back Cy Young Awards (he shared the '69 honor with Mike Cuellar).

At that point, McLain was 25 years old and had already amassed 108 wins in five years. Sadly, he went 17–34 over the next three years, including a 22-loss 1971 in which he bickered with Washington Senators manager Ted Williams the whole season.

McLain was out of baseball at 28, departing with a 131–91 record that covered 10 years.

MICKEY LOLICH, MCLAIN'S TEAMMATE in Detroit, had a thing for motorcycles. As a two-year-old, he drove his tricycle into a motorcycle, which fell on him and injured his left shoulder. That shoulder became famous when Lolich beat the Cardinals three times for Detroit to become the 1968 World Series MVP.

Lolich had a collection of motorcycles and frequently rode one of them to Tiger Stadium, putting his feet on the handlebars to avoid getting his trousers wet when he went through puddles.

The southpaw, who began with the Tigers in 1963, won at least 12 games every year from 1964–75, working more than 200 innings all 12 years. He pitched over 300 innings four years in a row, including 376 in 1971. Lolich led the American League in that category as well as wins (25), games started (45), complete games (29), and strikeouts (308), and finished second in the '71 Cy Young voting to **Vida Blue.**

THE 1968 WORLD SERIES, pitting the Tigers and Cardinals, was surprising in that it featured a pitching hero not named Gibson or McLain.

Both Cy Young Award winners started three games in the Series, and so did Lolich.

Gibson and McLain matched up in Game One, and it was a record-setting day for the St. Louis iron man. He struck out 17 (still the most ever in a World Series game) and threw a five-hitter in shutting out Detroit, 4–0. Lou Brock homered. McLain lasted five innings and took the loss.

Lolich pitched a complete game and hit the only home run of his 16-year career as the Tigers got even, 8–1. The first two games were in St. Louis.

Game Three moved to Detroit, where Tim McCarver and Orlando Cepeda belted three-run homers in a 7–3 St. Louis win. **Joe Hoerner** pitched three and two-thirds innings of scoreless relief to save it.

Mr. Gibson was back in control. He fanned 10, allowed five hits, and hit a home run. The 10–1 victory put the Cardinals up, 3–1, in the Series. Brock homered again.

St. Louis jumped to a 3–0 lead in the first as Orlando Cepeda clouted a two-run homer. Lolich threw blanks the rest of the way, while **Al Kaline** and Norm Cash drove in two runs apiece. The Tigers stayed alive, 5–3.

McLain finally pitched like an award-winner. He went the distance as Detroit evened the Series, crushing the Cards in St. Louis, 13–1. Kaline homered and knocked in four runs, Cash had two RBIs, and **Jim Northrup** blasted a grand slam.

Everything came down to Lolich and Gibson, Game Seven in St. Louis. It was scoreless until the seventh when Northrup ripped a two-run triple, followed by a Bill Freehan double.

Lolich came within an out of pitching a shutout, **Mike Shannon** spoiling it with a home run. The Tigers took it all, 4–1.

The southpaw was the Series MVP, but Detroit had a bunch of heroes. Kaline batted .379 with 8 RBIs, Northrup also driving in eight despite a .250 average. Cash hit .385 with five RBIs.

Brock led everyone with a .465 batting average. Cepeda drove in six runs. Gibson set a record by striking out 35 in a World Series. He pitched three complete games, as did Lolich. Both pitchers had a 1.67 earned run average for the Series.

JOHNNY BENCH BECAME THE PREMIER CATCHER in the majors almost overnight. Called up from Triple-A Buffalo in 1967, he caught 26 games for Cincinnati and was the Reds' starter behind the plate the next year as a 20-year-old.

He was an instant standout—a catcher who could handle pitchers, throw, and block bad balls, and who could hit for power and knock in runs—and was the National League's All-Star starter behind the plate from 1969–77.

The New York Yankees' Yogi Berra and the Brooklyn Dodgers' Roy Campanella glorified the catcher's position in the 1950s, when they each won three MVP awards, both getting their last in 1955.

By the time Bench came along, the Detroit Tigers' Bill Freehan was generally considered the top receiver in the big leagues. He hit 200 home runs and averaged 50 RBIs over a 15-year career.

Bench, who went on to slug 389 homers and drive in more than 100 runs six times, was the National League Most Valuable Player in 1970 and '72. Since then, only two catchers (the Yankees' **Thurman Munson** in 1976 and **Ivan Rodriguez** of the Texas Rangers in 1999) have been named MVP. Bench won 10 consecutive Gold Gloves.

STARTING IN 1968—Johnny Bench, Jerry Koosman, Stan Bahnsen, Del Unser, Ted Simmons, Ralph Garr, Bobby Cox, Bobby Bonds, Rollie Fingers, Richie Hebner, Hal McRae, Andy Messersmith.

Rookies of the Year were Bahnsen and Bench, the latter by one of the closest votes ever in the category.

Bench received 10.5 votes, Jerry Koosman 9.5 in balloting for the National League ROY award. Koosman won 19 games for the Mets and posted a 2.08 earned run average in 263 innings. Bench hit 15 home runs, had 82 RBIs, and batted .275 for the Reds, while serving notice that he was something special behind the plate.

McRae, who played for Kansas City his last 16 years, hit .290 lifetime. He had over 2,000 hits and nearly 500 doubles, including 54 in 1978. McRae batted over .300 six times, including '82 when he led the American League with 133 RBIs at the age of 36.

Bonds was ahead of his time. Long before batters were striking out with great frequency, Barry Bonds' dad was the Whiffmaster. He struck out every 4.6 trips to the plate over a 14-year career in which he also smacked also smacked 332 home runs.

Playing for eight teams, Bonds was a 30–30 guy four times and swiped more than 40 bases seven times, totaling 461. Bonds fanned over 100 times in a season 10 times, including back-to-back years with 187 and 189, the latter of which stood as the most in a season for a batter for decades.

Garr batted .306 over a 13-year career. His biggest seasons were with the Braves—.343 with 219 hits in 1971, National League-leading .353,

214 hits, and 17 triples in '74. Traded to Chicago, "The Roadrunner" hit .300 on the nose his first two years with the White Sox.

ENDING IN 1968—Rocky Colavito, Norm Siebern, **Russ Nixon**, **Floyd Robinson**, Elston Howard, Larry Jackson, Mickey Mantle, Roger Maris, Eddie Mathews, Stu Miller, **Larry Sherry**, Bill Virdon, **Bill Monbouquette**.

Colavito's last home run came against Cleveland, his original team and one whose fans adored him. He was traded after hitting 83 homers in two years and returned to the Indians, for whom he had his final big season.

In between, Colavito slugged 45 homers and drove in 140 runs for the 1961 Tigers. He had 374 career home runs and never struck out 100 times in a season.

Jackson won at least 13 games in 12 of his last 14 years in the majors, and hurled over 200 innings 11 times. Jackson won 24 for the 1964 Cubs.

Siebern batted .300 and won a Gold Glove his first full year in the big leagues. That was with the Yankees, who traded him to Kansas City. His best season was with the A's in 1962 when he hit .308 with 25 homers, 114 runs scored, 117 RBIs, and 110 walks.

Miller is remembered for being blown off the mound by a gust of wind in the 1961 All-Star Game in San Francisco, resulting in a "blown" save. The spindly right-hander was also famous for his effectiveness throwing slow, slower, and slowest.

Miller, who pitched until he was 40, started 93 games but is mostly known for coming out of the bullpen, which he did more than 600 times. He twice led the league in saves.

The 1959 World Series belonged to Larry Sherry. He earned two wins and two saves, posting a 0.71 earned run average, as the Dodgers defeated the Chicago White Sox in six games. Sherry had 82 career saves, 20 with Detroit in 1966.

LAST PITCH OF 1968 SEASON—Tigers Mickey Lolich to Tim McCarver in St. Louis. The Cardinals' catcher hit a foul popup that Detroit catcher Bill Freehan gathered in, closing the lid on a 4–1 Detroit win in Game 7 of the World Series.

Chapter 19

Four More Teams! Four More Teams!

The second wave of major league baseball expansion was not nearly as dramatic or eventful as the first. There was no threat of a new professional league to force the action, and there was no pressure to add a franchise in order to satisfy one city.

Instead, when four teams were added in 1969, the process was smooth. It was planned and scheduled, rather than occurring in shotgun fashion as had been the case eight years earlier. It wasn't as though expansion was casual, though.

Adding eight teams—an increase of 33 percent—in less than a decade was a very big deal. Especially after membership in the major league franchise owners' fraternity had remained at 16 for more than 60 years.

(Major league baseball doubled its number of teams after having eight in 1900. The 1901 season was the first with a National and American League, each with eight teams.)

While baseball's expansion late in the decade was not as emotional as the earlier enlargement, it was not without strong feelings. And, in fact, the '69 growth project to some degree was a reaction to other events in the world of professional sports.

The National Football League had become immensely popular across the country, and baseball knew it had to do something to remain the National Pastime. The NFL had recently merged with the AFL, expanding their geographic and marketing footprint.

That something was to get itself into more places, cities and venues, in order that more people could see the games and players. Availability meant getting out there.

Ever since the initial expansion, the major league hierarchy had been talking about the next one. In 1967, both leagues voted to add two teams each, bringing the overall total to 24, 12 in the National League and 12 in the American.

Buffalo, Dallas-Fort Worth, Denver, Oakland, San Diego, Seattle, and Toronto were most mentioned by those responding to a survey about possible locations for new teams. Milwaukee and New Orleans were among others.

Milwaukee had just lost the Braves to Atlanta in 1966 and would eventually land the Brewers. Toronto ended up with the Blue Jays down the road.

The 1969 newcomers were Seattle and Kansas City in the American League, San Diego and Montreal in the National.

Kansas City was home to the Athletics from 1955 until 1967, when they moved to Oakland. So the city was without a big league team for two years in the interlude. The new K.C. team was the Royals. Seattle kept a club for one year, after which the Pilots became the Brewers when relocating to Milwaukee.

Montreal's franchise was historic in that it was the first one to open shop outside United States borders. The San Diego Padres were part of the Pacific Coast League from 1936–68 and the very next year was part of the National League.

The expansion to 24 teams resulted in a reorganization of the major leagues. The American and National Leagues were each divided into two six-team divisions, necessitating playoff series that led to league championship series, which decided the pennants.

On October 14, 1968, an expansion draft was held for the Padres and Expos, with players chosen from the ten current National League teams. The next day, a draft was held for the Royals and Pilots, with players taken from a list made available by current American League teams.

The very first player selected was Giants outfielder **Ollie Brown**, taken by San Diego. The Padres then picked outfielder Manny Mota from the Pirates.

The first player to go in the AL draft was pitcher **Roger Nelson**, chosen by Kansas City from the Orioles. Then Seattle took first baseman Don Mincher from the Angels.

A pair of former MVP shortstops went No. 20 and No. 21 in the National League draft—Zoilo Versalles taken by San Diego from the Los Angeles Dodgers and Maury Wills grabbed by Montreal from Pittsburgh.

Other interesting names appearing on the expansion teams' first roster include the following:

Speedy outfielder Tommy Harper, by Seattle from Cleveland; one-time Dodgers star outfielder Tommy Davis, by Seattle from the Chicago White Sox; pitcher Wally Bunker, by Kansas City from Baltimore; outfielder **Lou Piniella**, by Seattle from Cleveland.

Lefty pitcher Steve Barber, by Seattle from the New York Yankees; folk hero/pitcher Moe Drabowsky, by Kansas City from Baltimore; ageless relief pitcher Hoyt Wilhelm, by Kansas City from the Chicago White Sox; Cy Young reliever Mike Marshall, by Seattle from Detroit.

Tommy Davis drove in 80 runs in only 123 games for the Seattle Pilots in 1969 before being traded to the Houston Astros just before the trade deadline.

Former hot outfield prospect Mack Jones, by Montreal from Cincinnati; eventual Reds pitching anchor **Jack Billingham**, by Montreal from the L.A. Dodgers; slugging first baseman Donn Clendenon, by Montreal from Pittsburgh; minor league first baseman **Nate Colbert**, by San Diego from Houston; longtime Cardinals and Cubs mound mainstay Larry Jackson, by Montreal from Philadelphia; one-time 20-game winner Mudcat Grant, by Montreal from the L.A. Dodgers; three-time .300 hitting outfielder **Tony Gonzalez**, by San Diego from Philadelphia.

Some of these names would find different rosters in a hurry. Wilhelm and Clendenon played key roles in the National League pennant race, with the latter shining on an even bigger stage before the final conclusion of the 1969 season.

There were other transactions as well. Jim Bouton, who won 21 games in a season for the Yankees, was sold by the Pinstripes to Seattle. Making more noise with his typing than his pitching, Bouton wrote plenty about the Pilots' one and only season and what went on in the clubhouse.

Although considered tattle tailing by major league players who felt their pranks and womanizing were sacred secrets, the Bouton's book *Ball Four* provided a new look at players as humans who did human—even if not always heroic—things away from the spotlights of big league stadiums.

In the first season with four six-team divisions, the newest clubs fared this way:

Kansas City finished fourth in the American League West, 69–93, 28 games behind first-place Minnesota. Seattle finished sixth (last) in the AL West, 64–98, 33 games behind the Twins. Montreal finished sixth in the National League East, 52–110, 48 games behind first-place New York. San Diego finished sixth in the NL West, 52–110, 41 games behind first-place Atlanta.

Gene Mauch, the longtime Phillies skipper, managed the Expos; **Preston Gomez** was the Padres' manager; Hall of Fame second baseman Joe Gordon managed the Royals; **Joe Schultz** was the Pilots' manager.

A few of the more memorable performances from 1969 expansion teams included Tommy Harper's 73 stolen bases for Seattle; Don Mincher's 25 home runs for Seattle; Gene Brabender's 13–14 record for Seattle; Mack Jones' 22 homers for Montreal; Moe Drabowsky's 11–9 with 11 saves for Kansas City; Rusty Staub's .302 average with 29 home runs for Montreal; Wally Bunker's 12–11 and 3.23 for Kansas City; and Nate Colbert's 24 home runs as a 23-year-old rookie first baseman for San Diego.

Colbert, who had 39 at-bats with Houston before being picked by the Padres, hit 38 homers in 1970 and totaled 163 in six years with San Diego. Amazingly, nearly 50 years since Colbert played, he remains the Padres' career home run leader.

Coco Laboy was an interesting choice by Montreal. The third baseman was a 28-year-old rookie out of the St. Louis Cardinals' organization. Laboy hit 18 homers and drove in 83 runs in 1969 and never approached those numbers again in parts of four seasons.

When the Pilots folded due to financial troubles, big league baseball returned to Milwaukee just four years after the Braves departed.

Of the eight teams joining the major leagues through expansion in the 1960s, five remain right where they started. The New York Mets, Houston Astros, California Angels, Kansas City Royals, and San Diego Padres.

The Angels, while staying in the same general vicinity, have been referred to as the Los Angeles Angels, California Angels, Los Angeles Angels of Anaheim, and the Anaheim Angels.

The Washington Senators became the Texas Rangers in 1972. The nation's capital got its third crack at a major league team when the Expos moved from Montreal to D.C. before the 2005 season. The nickname changed to Nationals, and they remain in Washington today. The Brewers are a long-running act in Milwaukee, having been there 48 years.

Chapter 20

1969: Looking for the Some Runs

The height of pitcher's mounds was not measured with any regularity until 1969. That was the first season after the rules committee made another set of changes involving pitchers.

The committee met in San Francisco following the 1968 season, with the goal to restore some offense to baseball. Owners wanted to put more fans in the seats, and it was their opinion that fans liked seeing runs scored and especially liked watching home runs being hit.

The general feeling was that fans looked at pitchers' duels and low-scoring games as boring, and that if the trend of pitching predominance continued, attendance would suffer.

So, mounds were lowered from 15 to 10 inches. Five inches, or one-third of the previous height, was an enormous reduction. The strike zone was also reduced, returning to the 1950 edict of armpits to the top of the knees.

There would also be more strict enforcement of rules prohibiting pitchers from using foreign substances on the ball. And, if a pitcher put his hand to his mouth while standing on the mound, a ball would be called.

Tony Cloninger, who won 57 games over a 3-year stretch for the Braves in the mid-1960s, felt the success of pitchers during the decade was due to a combination of factors.

"The widened strike zone helped," he said. "I know it helped me because control was never my strong point, and I needed all the strike zone I could get.

"The mounds were up there kind of high, and that was a big thing. You could really create a downward plane with the mounds that high. And the ballparks were a little bigger, so you could get away with some mistakes.

"The strike zone thing helped some pitchers more than others," Cloninger noted. "Any control pitcher gained more advantage. You take Warren Spahn; it had to be easier for him. If the umpires would give him an inch, he'd take two. If they'd give him two, he would take four.

"Spahnie would just keep going out there with that screwball of his. Juan Marichal was another one. He was so good at keeping the ball at the knees, and with the new rules, he got a whole lot of strikes below the knees.

"It wasn't that he didn't deserve it. Marichal could always pitch, and the bigger strike zone just helped him pitch even better."

Cloninger pitched three-and-a-half years in the Braves' minor league system before being brought up to Milwaukee in the middle of the 1961 season. The 20-year-old rookie could not have been more excited when he found his locker stuck right between Hank Aaron and Eddie Mathews.

"We had some great veteran pitchers on the Braves," Cloninger said. "Spahn, Burdette, Buhl . . . and those guys were really nice to me. They were happy and eager to answer my questions. They wanted to see me succeed.

"I learned from those guys, but I also learned a whole lot just sitting and listening to Aaron and Mathews.

"I probably learned as much from them as I did from anyone about how to pitch and what hitters look for in different situations. They didn't have all the computerized charts in the dugout like they do now. Those guys watched pitchers, stored information in their heads, and they didn't forget it.

"The rules weren't the reason for all the outstanding pitching," Cloninger said. "Bob Gibson was just so good that I don't care if it would have been today or when, he would have been great.

"In 1968, he just did whatever he wanted to do. Nobody could touch him. He was one tremendous pitcher. He knew what he was doing out there, he kept hitters off the plate, and then he kept the ball at the knees and on the corners."

"The lower mound was just a physical adjustment," Seaver said, "and I really don't remember anything about the strike zone being different . . . or, at least, changing anything for me.

"You always have to be able to adjust, and that was true with mounds because not all of them were the same. They were made of different compositions, so your landing area of your front foot was problematic. Los Angeles had a very heavy clay mound. Atlanta was very soft, so your foot would slide if your timing was incorrect.

"I can't remember any enforcement of the mound height, though," Seaver said. "I never saw or heard of anyone measuring mounds. The height of the mound depended on the pitching staff.

"Grounds crews always manicured the mound to suit the home team's pitchers. There were reports that the mound in L.A. was a little higher, and I wouldn't doubt that one iota."

Cloninger does not have fond memories of the 1968 rule changes. "When they lowered the mounds, that was the thing that hurt the most. It made a difference on your curve ball.

"They narrowed the strike zone, the ballparks started getting smaller, and later, the ball got livelier. It was a great time to be a hitter."

Bob Friend, like Seaver, worked 200 or more innings for 11 consecutive years. Friend was a workhorse for the Pittsburgh Pirates, with whom he spent all but one of his 16 seasons.

He won 197 games, including 22 in 1958 and 18 twice in the 1960s.

"I'm proud of the way I pitched," Friend said. "I went out there and took the ball—I didn't miss a start in 15 years—and I usually pitched far into the game.

"I didn't ask out of a start if I felt a little twinge or something in my arm. I always took my turn. I was fortunate not to have any serious arm problems, but I also pitched through some things. I think everybody who pitches has some soreness now and then; that's part of it.

"I think I was durable, both in terms of not missing starts and also in terms of pitching a lot of innings. I don't mean to put today's pitchers down, but back in the 1950s and 1960s, we didn't come out because we had thrown 100 pitches.

"I don't even think anybody was keeping count," Friend said with a chuckle. "We had to pitch out of a whole lot of jams because we didn't go to the bullpen as early or as often."

Cloninger, who had 67 wins by the time he was 25, knows about pitching with pain. "I had just had my best year in 1965 (24–11), and then we moved to Atlanta. I pitched on opening night in 1966, and I went 13 innings.

"The longest I had gone in spring training was six innings, and that opening game was on a cold April night, and it was kind of misting.

"That was the beginning of the end for me. I was so sore, and I wasn't feeling completely right when I came back at Shea Stadium a few days later.

"I kept taking my turn every fourth day, and it got to be really painful to pitch," Cloninger said. "It was like a knife cutting through my shoulder every time I went out.

"It was just survival after that. I never said anything to anybody. Guys didn't do that a whole lot back then. If you did, you would have been out of there as fast as you came in."

Cloninger pitched 257 innings that season, giving him 776 in three years. He pitched just 758 more innings over the last six years of his career, which concluded in 1972.

Fifteen years later, he began working in the minor leagues with the New York Yankees, and he was their pitching coach with the big club when it won four World Series championships under Joe Torre.

"The game has changed," Cloninger said. "It starts in the minor leagues where pitchers are only allowed to throw a limited number of pitches. Teams invest millions of dollars in these kids, and they are going to do everything possible to take care of them.

"Some of them come out of college and have to be rehabbed right away because they pitched so much for their schools. The complete game is rare now, but that's because nobody expects it.

"Starters are geared to go six or seven innings, then turn the game over to the set-up guys, and then you've got your closer.

"I do think baseball in the 1960s was special, but part of that was because it was when I played, and all of those big heroes I had read about were playing then.

"There were a whole bunch of great pitchers back then, and there are some mighty good arms now. Today's pitchers are just asked to do different things than they were when I played."

THE 1969 WORLD SERIES presented the classic mismatch. The mighty Baltimore Orioles with their glitzy offense and the not-quite-worst-to-first New York Mets with their gutsy, find-a-way style based on getting a couple of runs and holding 'em.

The Amazin's pitched 28 shutouts and won 41 one-run games. Cleon Jones batted .340, Tommie Agee hit 26 home runs, and they combined to score 189 runs and drive in 151. Tom Seaver won the Cy by going 25–7 with a 2.21, southpaw sidekick Jerry Koosman winning 17 with a 2.28.

Gary Gentry, a 22-year-old right-hander, was in the Mets' rotation all season. He made 35 starts, pitched 233 innings, had a 3.43 ERA, and pitched three shutouts, third on the team behind Koosman's six and five by Seaver.

Righty Ron Taylor and lefty Tug McGraw had nine wins apiece and combined for 25 saves. Nolan Ryan provided heat with more than a strikeout per inning.

The Mets hit 109 homers as a team. They added some pop in mid-June when they acquired first baseman Donn Clendenon from Montreal. The 6-foot-4 first baseman had a dozen home runs and 47 RBIs in his half-season with New York.

Baltimore, which won 109 games and won its division by 19 games, was loaded with power. 175 home runs, with Boog Powell slamming 37, the Robinsons (Frank 32, Brooks 23) teaming for 55, and center fielder extraordinaire Paul Blair adding 26.

The pitching staff had dual 20-game-winning lefties in Mike Cuellar and Dave McNally and right-hander Jim Palmer, who won 16 and had a 2.47 earned run average.

Everybody billed it David vs. Goliath at the ball yard. Things went according to script when Don Buford led off Game One with a home run off Seaver, who was outpitched by Cuellar, 4–1.

Koosman threw a 2-hitter over eight and two-thirds and got last-out help from Taylor in Game Two. Clendenon homered and Weis knocked in the game-winner with a ninth-inning single. 2–1, Mets.

Gary Gentry allowed three hits in six and two-thirds innings of Game Three. Nolan Ryan got a seven-out save with three strikeouts, and the Mets shut out the Orioles on four hits, 5–0.

Gentry, an .081 hitter during regular season, also drove in two second-inning runs with a double off Palmer. Agee led off the bottom of the first with a home run.

Ed Kranepool appeared in only one game of the 1969 World Series, but he made the most of it, cranking an 8th inning home run in the Mets' 5-0 Game 3 win. (National Baseball Hall of Fame and Museum).

Game Four was punctuated by Seaver's 10-inning six-hitter and The Catch. It was a game-saver made in right field by Ron Swoboda, an average defensive player whose first two big league hits were pinch-hit homers.

It was the ninth inning, with Seaver and the Mets nursing a 1–0 lead, compliments of a Clendenon home run. After one out, Frank Robinson singled and went to third on a base hit by Powell. Brooks Robinson came to the plate and lined a shot toward the gap in right-center field. It looked like extra bases and a Baltimore lead.

Swoboda ran over, dove and speared the ball backhanded as he sprawled in the Shea Stadium outfield grass. Frank Robinson scored the tying run, Brooks was credited with a sac fly, and **Elrod Hendricks** ended the inning with a line out.

When the Mets scored an unearned run in the bottom of the tenth, Seaver had a complete-game 2–1 victory, and New York was up, 3–1, in the Series.

Koosman survived home runs from Frank Robinson and McNally to go the distance for a 5–3 Game 5, Series-clinching win. Clendenon hit his third home run of the Series, a two-run shot, and Weis hit a game-tying homer in the seventh.

The Mets scored twice in the bottom of the eighth on doubles by Jones and Swoboda and another crucial Orioles error. When Koosman got a ground out and a couple of fly outs in the ninth, Shea Stadium went wild.

Clendenon was the Series MVP with his three home runs and four RBIs. Weis had five hits, three RBIs, and a .455 batting average.

STARTING IN 1969—Lou Piniella, **Carlos May, Ted Sizemore**, Al Oliver, **Larry Hisle, Mike Nagy, Bill Russell, Billy Conigliaro, Oscar Gamble**, Coco Laboy, **Bill Lee, Buck Martinez**.

Rookies of the Year were Piniella and Sizemore. Sizemore won the National League award handily, while Piniella received nine votes and Mike Nagy six.

Nagy went 12–2 with a 3.11 ERA for Boston, then managed eight wins over the last six years of his career.

Piniella played 18 years and had a .291 batting average. After being an everyday player for Kansas City, he had as many as 400 at-bats only three of 11 seasons with the Yankees.

A part-time left fielder most of his days with New York, "Sweet Lou" hit over .300 five times. He managed 23 years, taking the 1990 Cincinnati Reds to the World Series championship.

Oliver is one of the most accomplished hitters not in the Hall of Fame. He had over 2,700 hits and a .303 batting average in 18 years in the majors, hitting .300 or better 10 times.

At the age of 35, Oliver led the league in hitting at .331 and also with 204 hits, 43 doubles, and 109 RBIs. The seven-time All-Star never struck out more than 59 times in a season.

Lee won 119 games over 14 years, notching 17 three straight seasons in the mid-1970s for the Red Sox. "Spaceman" was always entertaining, a left-hander in every sense of the word.

Billy C. hit 18 home runs in 1970 and 40 in his five-year career. He was a teammate of brother Tony two seasons in Boston.

ENDING IN 1969—Don Drysdale, Buck Rodgers, Bill White, Ken Boyer, Bobby Cox, Johnny Podres, **Woodie Held**, Leon Wagner, **Ed Charles**, Jack Fisher, Tom Tresh, Lou Johnson.

Boyer was clutch in 11 years as the Cardinals' third baseman. He batted over .300 five times from 1956–61 and hit 18 or more home runs 10 years in a row, with a high of 32.

A seven-time All-Star and five-time Gold Glove winner, Boyer smacked 24 homers in both 1963 and '64, with respective RBI totals of 111 and 119. His 1964 MVP performance was capped by two home runs in the Cards' World Series victory over the Yankees.

Fisher is remembered most for giving up Ted Williams' career-concluding home run. That was in 1960, which turned out to be the right-hander's best season—a 12–11 record and 3.41 ERA. Fisher had the misfortune of pitching for the then pitiful Mets and was saddled with 73 losses in four years, including 24 in 1965.

Cox's playing career was done after two seasons, both with the Yankees. A third baseman, he hit nine home runs and batted .225 in 628 at-bats. The Hall of Fame manager had 2,504 wins in 29 years, guiding the Braves to five pennants, a World Series title, and those amazing 14 consecutive division championships.

Wagner hit the long ball. He cracked 51 home runs in the Carolina League in 1956, then hit 211 in 12 big league seasons. "Daddy Wags" had 37 homers and 107 RBIs for the 1962 Los Angeles Angels, placing him fourth in the American League MVP voting.

Held played for seven teams in a 14-year career, beginning with the Yankees and ending with the White Sox. He hit 130 of his lifetime 179 home runs in seven seasons with the Indians, playing shortstop, second and third base, and in the outfield. Held hit 20 or more homers four times.

LAST PITCH OF 1969 SEASON—Mets Jerry Koosman to Baltimore's Davey Johnson. The Orioles' second baseman flied out to deep left field, Cleon Jones making the catch just short of the Shea Stadium warning track. That concluded a 5–3 New York World Series-clinching win in Game 5.

Chapter 21

More Essential '60s Stories

Wonderful Willie

Any conversation about baseball in the 1960s probably should start with Willie Mays. In fact, his name could arguably headline anything said or written about the history of major league baseball.

Certainly, it is difficult to dispute a claim that he is the greatest all-around player. Babe Ruth has to be right there at the top because of his dominance as a pitcher before assuming the throne as the game's premier power hitter.

While Mays never took the mound, his speed and the way he used it elevated his stature among the all-time great superstars. Stealing bases was not the rage when he played, though he did his share of that.

It was his ability to run down balls in center field that added extra stars to Mays' crown, while preventing runs in bunches. Turning would-be extra-base hits into routine outs, he made difficult plays look easy.

Mays was voted the National League Most Valuable Player twice (1954 and 1965) in his 22-year career. He deserved several more, but was so good for so long, his greatness became nearly taken for granted. He finished in the top five in the balloting seven additional times and was sixth three times.

Mays was a dominant player for 18 years—from his age-23 MVP 1954 season, through 1971, when he was 40 and led the National League on on-base average and chalked up a dazzling WAR of 6.3 (calculated retroactively). He was a strong MVP contender 12 of the 18 years.

By the time the 1960s arrived, The Say Hey Kid was a superstar with six outstanding seasons under his belt. During the 1960s, Mays batted .300, slammed 350 home runs, drove in 1,003 runs, and had 1,635 hits, 662 (40 percent) of which went for extra bases.

He hit 40 or more homers four times, with a career-high 52 in 1965, and had 100 or more RBIs seven consecutive seasons, with a career-high 141 in 1962. Mays also scored 100 or more runs for 12 consecutive seasons, from 1954-1965, surpassing 120 in six of those seasons.

Mays was the National League MVP in 1965 when he hit .317, blasted 52 home runs, and had 112 RBIs. From 1960–66, his MVP vote placings were: third, sixth, second, fifth, sixth, first, third.

Mays' 7,095 putouts are the most by an outfielder in major league history. He hit 660 home runs, had 3,283 hits, scored 2,062 runs, and drove in 1,903, while batting .302 over a 22-year career. The 1951 Rookie of the Year and '54 MVP was a 20-time All-Star who won 12 straight Gold Gloves.

But there was much more to this richly talented player than his astounding numbers. His energy and enthusiasm combined to form an electricity, one that jolted teammates, opposing players, and fans.

Especially fans. They got something special for the price of a ticket to a Giants game when Willie Mays was playing. He might go 0-for-3 and be what everybody talked about that night.

Because he would dash from first to third on a single (losing his hat on the way), then score the go-ahead run in a cloud of dust on a short fly to the outfield.

For good measure, he would save the lead and the game with one of his Jesse Owens dashes into the gaps of right- or left-center. Arriving in time to make a routine catch. Routine for Willie Mays.

There was no accounting for the value of Mays in a particular game or over a season by simply studying the box scores. They didn't show how great a catch was, or a throw that wasn't an assist but prevented a runner from moving up, or an extra base he took.

Mays hit for average and for power, he ran fast, he could field, and he could throw. But he was a six-tool player instead of five. Because, in addition to tremendous skills, he possessed an instinct and the ability to anticipate that led to feats that went beyond even his extraordinary abilities.

Oliva's Cooperstown Trip Hijacked

Tony Oliva appeared destined for the Hall of Fame when he sprinted onto the major league scene. And he might have made it if not for seven knee operations that forced him to limp through his last five seasons.

Oliva broke into the big leagues with a big bang as he led the American League in hitting his first two years.

In 1964, The Minnesota Twins right fielder put up astounding numbers, which included leading the league with 217 hits, 43 doubles, 374 total bases, and a .323 batting average. He added 32 home runs and 94 RBIs.

As a result, Oliva was a landslide choice as Rookie of the Year. For an encore, he hit .321, with 40 doubles, 16 homers, and a team-leading 98 RBIs as the Twins won the American League pennant. Oliva finished second in the 1965 American League Most Valuable Player voting behind teammate Zoilo Versalles.

The next year, Oliva kept it up, hitting .307 with 25 homers.

Then knee problems began. He had surgery to repair torn ligaments in his right knee in 1967 and '68, slowing Tony considerably (whose actual name is Pedro) as his batting average dipped to .289 both years.

Bouncing back, he hit over .300 in 1969 and '70, averaging 200 hits, 23 home runs, and 104 RBIs for the two seasons. 1971 was a good and bad year for Oliva. He won his third batting title with a career-high .337, but tore cartilage in his right knee.

After that, Oliva was never the same. Undergoing seven knee operations in seven years, Oliva played in only 10 games in 1972 and was strictly a designated hitter his final four seasons.

But, oh, those first eight years were glorious. The left-handed-hitting line drive machine averaged 182 hits, 22 home runs, and a .313 batting mark, and he was an All-Star each of those seasons. Hall of Fame stuff to be sure, but not enough years to build lifetime numbers worthy of standard election.

In 2015, Oliva and Dick Allen both fell one vote short of election by the Golden Era Committee.

The Dynasty That Wasn't

One of the real surprises of the 1960s was the disappearance of the Braves. From Milwaukee and from the annual National League pennant chase.

The Braves' move from Boston to Milwaukee for the 1953 season was joyously received at County Stadium. The Braves led the National League in attendance that year and for the next five, averaging more than two million fans for six years.

From that point, it was a steady drop as crowds grew smaller each season. The team drew under a million people for the first time in its 10-year Milwaukee stay with a figure of just under 767,000 in 1962. Four years later, the Braves were calling Atlanta home.

Dynasty is a word that comes to mind when thinking about the Milwaukee Braves of the late 1950s. They came within two wins of being mentioned in conversations of major league teams that dominated for a while.

The Braves finished one game behind the Brooklyn Dodgers in the 1956 National League standings. Milwaukee won the next two NL pennants, by a comfortable eight games both times, and split two World Series with the New York Yankees.

In 1959, the Braves and Los Angeles Dodgers were tied atop the standings after the regular season, L.A. sweeping two straight from Milwaukee in the playoff series.

Entering the 1960s, there were numerous good reasons to believe the Braves would continue to be a contender. Their names were Aaron, Mathews, Spahn, Burdette, Crandall, and Adcock.

The core of the team was young. Mathews was 28, Aaron 26, six-time All-Star catcher Del Crandall 30, and there was a 19-year-old star catcher in waiting named Joe Torre. Plus, the Big Three of Warren Spahn, Lew Burdette, and Bob Buhl were all pitching very well.

The Braves made some noise in 1960 and did manage to finish second behind the Pittsburgh Pirates, albeit seven games back. The next year, Milwaukee finished fourth, then no higher than fifth seven years in a row.

The once powerful and not all that long ago borderline dominant team became a perennial mediocre club that flirted with or lived in the second division.

What in the world happened? It wasn't Spahn's fault. The lefty who looked old but pitched young (he turned 39 at the start of the '60 season) won 83 games over four years.

His sidekick and partner in pranks, Burdette, won 47 games in three seasons before being traded. Buhl was a 16-game winner in 1960, struggled the next season, and was shipped to the Cubs the first month of the '62 season.

Neither right fielder Aaron nor third baseman Mathews was to blame. They combined to hit 79, 66, 74, and 67 home runs from 1960–63.

Joe Adcock, the first baseman from Louisiana, was still doing his part, with 99 homers in three years—until the Braves mysteriously decided to get rid of him. They traded Adcock to Cleveland in November, 1962, and got basically nothing in return.

All those years squatting behind the plate began to take a toll on Crandall. The four-time Gold Glove winner missed most of 1961 with a shoulder injury, and after the '62 season, he became Torre's backup before being traded.

The middle infield got too old. Second baseman Red Schoendienst and shortstop Johnny Logan both were done in Milwaukee by the end of the '60 season.

Schoendienst was sent to St. Louis, where he had flourished as a youngster, making nine All-Star teams. Logan lost his starting job in 1961 and was dealt to Pittsburgh in June.

By 1963, Aaron and Mathews were the only two position players' names left from the Braves' lineup card presented to umpires at the start of the decade.

Spahn was the starting pitcher for that same lineup, and he was magnificent in '63, but even he proved mortal the next year at the age of 43. The southpaw was gone by 1964, the last of the Big Three to be traded.

Center fielder and leadoff man Billy Bruton, known for his speed, his strong faith in God, and for being a father figure to many of his teammates, was gone after the 1960 season.

Bruton was traded to Detroit despite a season that included career highs in extra-base hits and runs scored. Mathews, whose last good year was 1965, was swapped to Houston on New Year's Eve, 1966.

The mighty Braves, who had thrilled fans in County Stadium and struck fear into the hearts of the rest of the National League, were no more. The rebuilt version, Atlanta emblazoned on jerseys where Milwaukee used to be, did vault from fifth place the previous season to win the West in 1969.

The new Braves—Orlando Cepeda coming over from St. Louis to join Aaron, Felipe Alou, Rico Carty, and **Clete Boyer**—were swept by

East Division champ New York in three straight in the National League Championship Series.

But at least the Braves managed a first-place finish during the 1960s after so much futility. And after so much was expected of them, especially from themselves.

As to why the plague of mediocrity struck such a talented team which was still relatively young, the culprit was the one most common to baseball shortcomings.

Pitching, or rather, the lack of it. After posting either the first- or second-best earned run average in the National League from 1956–59, the Braves ranked no better than fourth throughout the '60s. They fell all the way to ninth (ahead of only the New York Mets) in 1964.

The next time a Braves hurler pitched like an ace was when Phil Niekro was a 23-game winner in 1969. Coincidentally (or not), the Braves won a title of any kind for the first time in 11 years.

Aaron and Mathews: Dynamite Duo

The story is told of the time during the 1958 World Series when Henry Aaron walked to the plate, and Yankees catcher Yogi Berra advised him to turn the bat around so he could read the label (in order to prevent breaking his bat).

Aaron's paraphrased reply was that he wasn't up there to read, he was up there to hit.

Which was always the case, and no one did it better. Lifetime batting averages might not agree, but two statistics, one of them vastly overlooked, reveal just how well Aaron hit.

He is the all-time leader in total bases with 6,856 and in runs batted in with 2,297. Total bases are not always discussed vigorously among everyday fans, but it is by those who follow the game closely and who scrutinize numbers.

One thing a lofty total bases figure says is that the hitter frequently put himself in scoring position. Aaron had 3,771 hits, 1,477 — 39 percent — of which were for extra bases.

A .305 career hitter, The Hammer never struck out 100 times in a season. He averaged only 60 whiffs over 23 years, just once every nine at-bats, and reached base 37 percent of the time. From 1955–63, he averaged 196 hits per season.

Aaron was the National League Most Valuable Player in 1957, when he led the Milwaukee Braves to the pennant and a World Series win over the Yankees. He finished third in the MVP voting six times.

He led the league at least twice in runs, hits, doubles, home runs, RBIs, batting average, slugging percentage, and total bases during his career. The fact that much of Aaron's prime was spent during a pitching-dominated era, makes his numbers that much more impressive.

Despite the fact that Barry Bonds' career stat sheet shows him with 762 home runs, Aaron's 755 continue to warrant his more than casual recognition as major league baseball's home run king.

He never hit the 50 mark in homers but had 40 or more eight times, with a high of 47 at the age of 37. He hit 44—his uniform number—four times.

In 1959, Aaron established career highs with 223 hits, a .355 average, and 400 total bases. That followed a '57 World Series highlighted by three home runs and seven runs driven in, numbers he matched in just three games in Atlanta's 1969 NLCS loss to the New York Mets.

Those who go back far enough likely associate the term Dynamic Duo with Batman and Robin. Longtime baseball fans associate it with Ruth and Gehrig. Those who examine numbers more closely might say Aaron and Mathews.

Based strictly on home run totals, that would be the best association. For their careers, Hank Aaron (755) and Eddie Mathews (512) combined to hit more home runs than anybody, 1,267. Sixty more than Babe Ruth (714) and Lou Gehrig (493).

As Braves, Aaron (733) and Mathews (493) had 1,226 homers, while as Yankees, Ruth (659) and Gehrig (493) had 1,152.

As teammates, the homer totals are very close. Playing together with the Milwaukee and Atlanta Braves for 13 years (1954–66), Aaron (442) and Mathews (421) combined to hit 863 home runs. Playing together with the New York Yankees for 12 years (1923–34), Ruth (511) and Gehrig (348) had 859.

Eddie Mathews surpassed 100 walks in five different seasons, leading the league in that category four times. (National Baseball Hall of Fame and Museum).

Certainly there was no more prolific pair than the Braves' sluggers from the mid-1950s to the mid-'60s. During a 10-year stretch from 1954-1963, they combined for 685 home runs and 2,229 RBIs. Those figures far outdistanced Mickey Mantle and Yogi Berra of the Yankees, who totaled 561 home runs and 1,708 RBIs for the same period (Mantle 362–943; Berra 199–765).

No hitter was better overall in the 1960s than Aaron. He was 26 years old when the decade began and 35 when it ended. During that period, he amassed 375 home runs, 3,343 total bases and 1,107 RBIs, with a .308 batting average.

Mathews is remembered for being the cover boy of the first-ever edition of Sports Illustrated magazine. And for recording the final out of the 1957 World Series, wrapping up Milwaukee's victory over the Yankees.

The Hall of Fame third baseman is also remembered for slamming 47 home runs as a 21-year-old, adding 135 RBIs and a .302 batting average in a 1953 season that earned him a second-place MVP finish behind Roy Campanella.

Mathews followed with 40 homers the next year and 41 in '55, giving him 153 at the age of 23. He slugged 46 home runs and drove in 114 in 1959, carrying him to another MVP runner-up, this time behind Ernie Banks.

Mathews had hit 370 homers before he was 30. He ended with 512, with just 35 in his last three seasons. He was a part-timer on the Detroit team that lost to St. Louis in the 1968 World Series.

Acknowledging that Mathews was a terrific lineup comrade, it must be emphasized that his production waned drastically as the '60s wound down. After 1961, when he was only 30, he never hit as many as 30 home runs in a season, and he didn't hit the 100-RBI mark after 1960, when he was 28.

Sixties Cy to Marichal

They should have given Juan Marichal a Cy Young Award for the 1960s. The entire decade. Despite winning more games than any pitcher during the '60s, Marichal never received a vote in the decade's annual Cy balloting. Not one! In fact, he got only one Cy Young vote during his 14 full years in the majors, and that was in 1971.

It is easy to take either side in the argument whether Bob Gibson or Marichal was the "best" pitcher of the '60s. Both have glowing numbers to support them.

Gibson was a unanimous Cy Young selection in 1968. So was Sandy Koufax in 1963, '65, and '66. The Dodgers' left-hander isn't mentioned in the same Best of '60s conversation with Marichal and Gibson because he did not pitch the last three years of the decade.

(A note on the Cy Young Award. Only one was given until 1967, the first year a pitcher was recognized in both leagues.)

Characterized by his high leg kick, pinpoint control, and multiple delivery angles for his pitches, Marichal led the National League with 191 wins from 1960–69. Bob Gibson was a distant second with 163.

Marichal was a 20-game winner six times—all in the '60s—and led the National League with 25 victories in 1963 and 26 in 1968. His 2.10 earned run average led the league in 1969, and his ERA was under 2.50 five other times during the decade.

For those 10 years, his ERA was 2.57. Gibson's was 2.74. Marichal struck out 1,840 batters in 2,549 and two-thirds innings during the '60s, Gibson 2,071 in 2,447 innings. Marichal pitched 45 shutouts, Gibson 42.

When Gibson had The Year in 1968, Marichal had a pretty astounding year of his own. What was phenomenal about the St. Louis right-hander's season were his microscopic 1.12 ERA and his 13 shutouts. Marichal's 1968 numbers included 26 wins, 30 complete games, and 325 and two-thirds innings pitched.

Yet, when Marichal's name comes up in discussing the 1960s, the thing often remembered is what he did with a bat, not his arm. Naturally, it involved the Dodgers.

Brock's Sensational Series Success

Lou Brock has always dashed to the next base. Whether stealing one, as he did 938 times during a 19-year major league career, or establishing one in his role as a diabetes advocate.

In early 2016, the Hall of Fame outfielder predicted that he would soon be back to full speed. He was recovering from surgery the previous fall in which his left leg was amputated below the knee. The reason was an infection resulting from diabetes.

Brock is one of the all-time most successful World Series performers, one who was able to rise above his already expansive capacity for hitting and stealing bases.

He gathered more than 3,000 hits and over 900 steals, while scoring more than 1,600 runs. He had some pop, too, smacking 149 home runs and driving in 900 runs.

Now, Brock's regular-season stats are glowing, they really lit up in October. The Fall Classic was his time. In three World Series, all in the '60s, he piled up 34 hits, 16 runs, and 13 RBIs, batting first or second for the Cardinals.

He stole 14 bases in 16 tries, clouted four home runs, and had seven doubles. His 21-game Series batting average is .391, with .424 and .655 on-base and slugging percentages, respectively.

From the time St. Louis got him in a trade in 1964, Brock was consistent. He pounded out 193 or more hits eight times, including six in a row when he was 30–35 years of age. He scored over 100 runs seven times and stole 12 consecutive seasons, with a high of 118, which he accomplished when he was 35.

The World Series was no different for Brock. In the brightest spotlight, with pressure at a fever pitch, he produced. He had at least one hit in 16 of 21 Series games, including his last nine.

The best of three seven-game Series was his final one, 1968, when the Cardinals lost to the Tigers. Brock batted .464 with 13 hits that included three doubles, a triple, and two home runs. He swiped seven bases, scored six runs, and knocked in five.

Ducky Personified 1960 Bucs

The 1960 world champion Pittsburgh Pirates were a team without stars, a bunch of guys who liked each other, got along in the clubhouse, and picked one another up.

Dick Schofield was the perfect example.

Coming off the bench is a difficult job in any sport. In baseball, the task can be daunting when it involves going up to the plate cold and facing a pitcher who has been on fire or having to make a difficult play on defense right away.

One at-bat or a few innings, and it's normally back to the pines until the next call comes from the manager. That may take a day, or two, or a week. And that's tough.

So is being called upon to replace a regular position player who is injured. While everyone yearns for the chance to play every day, the circumstances surrounding that opportunity can be overwhelming.

Take Schofield in 1960, for example.He was the Pittsburgh Pirates' utility infielder, and a darn good one. Primarily a shortstop throughout his major league career, he could play second base and third equally well. He had outstanding range, a strong arm, good feet, and he could make the pivot on the double play from short or second. He could make all the plays.

Hitting, or a lack of it for most of his time in the majors, was another story, the main reason Schofield was not somebody's everyday shortstop. Which he was for a few of his big league seasons.

A switch-hitter, who was five-foot-nine and weighed around 160 pounds, he was good bunter who tried to put the ball in play, advance runners, and just get on base.

On September 6, 1960, when Dick Groat had his wrist broken by a Lew Burdette pitch, the Pirates' shortstop job was Schofield's. While there weren't any rah-rahs or go-get-'ems from his teammates, they knew the man called Ducky was more than adequate with the glove.

"Ducky" was a nickname Schofield inherited from his dad, who was affectionately called that by folks in the town of Marcus Hook—near

Chester, Pennsylvania—where he grew up. Some of Schofield's teammates heard him call his dad Ducky and started calling him the same thing.

Schofield slid comfortably into the eighth spot in the Pittsburgh batting order and into the left side of the infield, with Don Hoak on one side of him and Bill Mazeroski on the other.

He entered the lineup as a pinch-hitter for Groat, who was unable to continue after his right wrist had swollen. It was the bottom of the third inning, there was one out, no one was on base, and the game with Milwaukee was scoreless.

Hitting .200 for the season, Schofield singled to right field and promptly scored on a double by **Bob Skinner**. The Bucs went on to win, 5–3, as Schofield went 3-for-3 and started a double play in the field.

He got a hit in the next game and the one after that, eventually hitting in his first six games after taking over for the Pirates' captain. After a couple of hitless games, Schofield put together an eight-game hitting streak.

In a stretch of 21 games, Schofield had one or more hits in 17 of them, went 27-for-67 for a .403 batting average, scored four runs, and batted in nine.

He had four doubles, a triple, drew eight walks, and had a .467 on-base percentage. He handled 105 chances and made two errors for a .981 fielding percentage and was involved in 15 double plays.

"It was a fantastic time," Schofield said. "Things worked out pretty well. We lost a really good player and a leader when Groat went down.

"Nobody likes to see someone get hurt, especially one of your key players when you're in a pennant race. But it was an opportunity for me to play.

"I know the team needed me to play well, but really, everyone needed to play well. That's the way it is when you're a contending team. Especially when you don't have one or two big guns you're depending on.

"What we did in 1960 was a team thing in every sense," Schofield pointed out. "Different guys coming through every day. We didn't have one player we depended on.

"That's why, even though Dick was having a great year and he was one of our key players, there wasn't a burden on me to do what he had been doing.

"I don't remember thinking I was on the spot or anything like that," Schofield said. "I know (manager Danny) Murtaugh and the players never gave me the feeling that there was pressure on me to do certain things.

"As a shortstop, you always know the main thing is to make the plays, the routine plays. I knew I could do that. I was always confident in my ability to catch and throw the ball. I could field, and I had a good arm."

"As for the hitting, I'm sure I surprised some people. And I'm not going to say I could do that over an entire season. Nobody could, except for Ted Williams.

"When you bat eighth, as I did, you can do a couple of things that really help the club. There are chances to drive in a few runs, and then, you want to keep innings alive so, at the very least, the team is back to the top of the order the next inning. I thought I did both of those things fairly consistently.

"It felt good," Schofield said, "to have helped us, helped us win some games down the stretch. There wasn't a lot said about it, nor should there have been. I was just doing my job, and I'm glad I could do it well.

"Was I proud? I don't know about that. Like I have said, everyone on that team did his job. I think I was most proud to be a part of that team because it really was such a great bunch of men."

Flood Turns the Tide Forever

Stories are told of Mickey Mantle tooth-grinding meetings with George Weiss during which he asked for pay raises. Despite big seasons with big numbers, the Mick would be turned down by the Yankees' general manager. Or given a piddling increase.

That was before Curt Flood and Marvin Miller. Back when players had no leverage. Or options. They took what ownership would pay or they could find a new job. "Holding out" did little to change management's mind because both sides knew it was just a matter of time before the player gave in.

Sometimes there might be a little crack in a GM's armor, with a resulting small raise in salary. Never, however, was it in proportion to the player's increase in production the previous season. Not to mention, general managers took every opportunity to reduce salaries.

A dip in performance, even if the numbers were still outstanding, often resulted in a dip in pay.

Along came Curt Flood and his willingness to be a sacrificial lamb, and Marvin Miller with his skills in establishing bargaining power, and the table was leveled. Even tilted toward the players after forever having been practically vertical in its slant toward ownership.

When you think back to pre-free-agency days and before television poured zillions of dollars into major league coffers, salaries were skimpy and even superstars did not make huge bucks.

Looking at today's pay days and long-term contracts, one can't help but wonder what it would take to sign a Mantle, Mays, Koufax, or Aaron. A well stocked bank vault and half ownership of a team might not be far-fetched.

The way it was would be the way it remained if left up to the owners. They did not open their checkbooks out of generosity or a desire to "treat our players right."

Two men paved the road to players' freedom to make their own deals and choose their teams rather than labor in servitude, with sarcastic laments from the front office similar to what Weiss once told Mantle: (paraphrased) "If you don't sign, what are you going to do—go work in the mines with your dad?"

Watching Curt Flood play center field for the High Point-Thomasville Hi-Toms in the summer of 1956 was both a treat and a great deception.

He was such a gifted and entertaining player that he made baseball look too easy.

Displaying sprinter's speed, Flood covered the spacious outfield almost from one foul line to the other. His corner-outfield teammates stayed out of the way, happy to let him run down everything hit in the air.

And he did. Flood was heroic at the bat as well as in the field. Playing in all 154 games, he had 190 hits, slugged 29 home runs, and had 317 total bases.

The Carolina League Player of the Year for the first-place Hi-Toms, he was obviously headed for the Big Time. He got there quickly, getting the September cup of coffee with Cincinnati that year and another one the next season.

In 1958, Flood was up for good. But with St. Louis as the Reds had traded him in December. He was the Cardinals' center fielder most of the next three seasons, but never really got going.

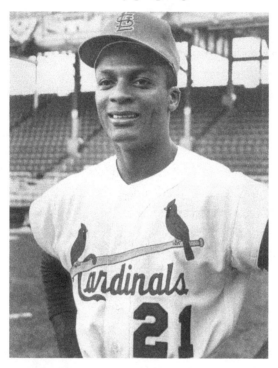

Curt Flood won the Gold Glove for his play in center field each of his last seven years with the Cardinals. (National Baseball Hall of Fame and Museum).

He batted over .300 in '61, but in fewer than 350 at-bats. Flood took off the next year, hitting .296 with 188 hits. He averaged 200 hits and above .300 from 1963–65, when he was in center field just about every day for St. Louis.

Flood was outstanding in all three of the Cardinals' pennant winning years of the decades, batting .311 in 1964, .335 in '67, and .301 in '68. He made three All-Star teams and won seven straight Gold Gloves.

After Flood's average dipped to .285 in 1969, St. Louis traded him in October. Tried to, anyway. The Cards announced a deal that would send Flood, Tim McCarver, Joe Hoerner, and **Byron Browne** to Philadelphia for Dick Allen, **Cookie Rojas**, and **Jerry Johnson**.

Except that Flood didn't want to go. He wrote a letter to Commissioner Bowie Kuhn, essentially asking to become a free agent. When Kuhn rejected the request, Flood sued him and Major League Baseball, saying its reserve clause violated antitrust laws and the Thirteenth Amendment, which barred slavery.

(The reserve clause said major league players were "owned" by teams, an individual bound to his team as long as the team wanted. There was no recourse. A player could not leave one team and sign with another.)

The case went to the Supreme Court, which ruled in favor of MLB, 5–3. Two years later, the decision was reversed, dispensing with the reserve clause and paving the way for free agency as we know it today.

Although what he did made modern players rich and free to ultimately play for a team of their choice, Flood paid dearly.

His playing career was finished. He was 31 when traded, pretty much in his prime. The Phillies swapped him to the Washington Senators, and he played 13 games for them in 1971 before retiring.

Flood was not the same player he had been. The ordeal took a huge toll on him emotionally and financially as well. He was left with little money and struggled until dying in 1997.

He had a .293 lifetime batting average and nearly 1,900 hits in 12 full big league seasons. Admirable numbers. But Curt Flood is best remembered as being the father of free agency.

The Revolution That Was Marvin Miller

THE BASEBALL HALL OF FAME membership includes former managers, general managers, writers, and broadcasters in addition to players. Also umpires, league presidents, and commissioners.

But the man who did more than anyone for players does not have a plaque at Cooperstown. And it is a glaring omission.

Marvin Miller served as the director of the Major League Baseball Players Association (MLBPA) for seventeen years (1966–82), and during that time he transformed it into one of the most powerful unions in the United States.

A negotiator and vital cog of the United Steelworkers, Miller was elected executive director of the MLBPA in the spring of 1966. Within two years, he helped win players a minimum salary increase of nearly forty-three percent while also setting the stage for better player-owner relations, which up to that time had practically been non-existent.

Miller effectively and affectively led negotiations, precipitated by bold stands against the owners that included a players strike in 1981.

By the time free agency was in place and he had retired, the average player's annual salary had risen from $19,000 to $326,000. Two years later, again as a result of Miller's laying the foundation, arbitration became a vehicle for players to have salary demands subjected to an impartial third party.

Despised by owners, Miller has not been elected to the Hall of Fame, in large part because voting bodies were loaded with front-office types. Based on his contribution to the game, one would have to say his treatment has been unfair.

Renowned baseball broadcaster Red Barber cited Miller, along with Babe Ruth and Jackie Robinson as the "most important men in baseball history." Former Major League Baseball Commissioner Fay Vincent called Miller "the most important baseball figure of the last fifty years."

Miller emancipated the players, and that is what riled the owners. Baseball was not their game any more, once the MLBPA took hold. The players suddenly had rights. And power.

Imagine that, after all those years of having none of either.

The owners could not accept it, though they had to deal with it. Still, they viewed Marvin Miller as the enemy and never forgave him. So they have done all they could to keep him out of Cooperstown.

They Called It "The Holdout"

In February of 1966, the Twin Towers of pitching joined together to announce they would refuse to report to spring training with the Los Angeles Dodgers unless and until their combined salary demands were met.

Sandy Koufax and Don Drysdale initially asked for a million dollars over three years, divided equally. That came to $167,000 per year per pitcher. Pennies in this day's MLB market when considering the average salary is millions.

Public sentiment was not on the pitchers' side, despite their immense popularity and success. Remember, Sandy and Double D were stars. Big stars.

Most people felt professional athletes were lucky to be playing a game for a living instead of having to work "real jobs," and that they should be grateful for whatever they were paid.

The pitchers certainly had leverage and plenty of it.

Koufax had won 26 games in 1965, earning the National League Cy Young Award and finishing second to Willie Mays in the Most Valuable Player voting. Drysdale was a 23-game winner in '65 and also swung a potent bat, hitting .300 with seven home runs. He placed seventh on the MVP ballot.

Koufax had been paid $85,000 in 1965, Drysdale $80,000. The Dodgers offered to raise Koufax to $100,000 and Drysdale to $85,000 for the '66 season. The dual holdout was, and is, unprecedented.

The drama ended on March 30, 1966, when they signed, Koufax for $125,000 and Drysdale for $110,000. Neither received a multi-year contract, though the '66 season was Koufax's last, anyway.

Brooklyn's Final Chapter

The storybook that was the Brooklyn Dodgers wrote its final chapter during the 1960s, marking the close of one of the most beloved franchises in major league history.

Ebbets Field, perhaps the closest thing to a community center of any ballpark in any sport at any time, had been bulldozed in 1960. By 1969, every last one of the Dodgers who beat the Yankees in that landmark 1955 World Series were out of baseball as players.

In addition, all but one of the players who had spent time on the Dodgers' roster during the 1957 season, their last in Brooklyn, were gone from the game by '69. The exception was John Roseboro, whose final season was 1970.

Reese, Robinson, Campanella, Snider, Hodges, Newcombe, and Furillo were the best remembered names from the Brooklyn team that won five National League pennants in a six-year span (the 1954 New York Giants interrupted the Dodger dominance from 1951–56).

Jackie Robinson, Roy Campanella, and Pee Wee Reese were out of baseball by the end of the 1950s, with Carl Furillo, and Don Newcombe finished by the end of 1960 season.

The Dodgers had traded Newcombe during the 1958 season, made Gil Hodges available in the 1961 expansion draft, and sold Duke Snider in the spring of '63.

Robinson retired before the 1957 season rather than join the dreaded Giants in a trade. Campanella's career ended with a tragic automobile accident prior to the 1958 season that left the great catcher in a wheelchair for the rest of his life. Reese called it quits after a '58 season in which he played in only 59 games.

Big Newk was a three-time 20-game winner, including 1956 when his 27 victories propelled him to the Cy Young and National League Most Valuable Player awards. He took the ball. For a period of seven seasons, the right-hander averaged 233 innings.

Frequently used as a pinch-hitter, Newcombe hit 15 career home runs, and in 1955, he batted .359 with seven homers and 23 RBIs. His lifetime batting average was .271.

He was 0–6 when the Dodgers traded him to Cincinnati in June of 1958. Newcombe was a 13-game winner the next year for the Reds. They sold him to Cleveland in 1960, and he finished the year and his career with the Indians.

After averaging 30 home runs during an 11-year period, Hodges hit only eight in 1960 and again in '61. He was 37 years old, and he was draft bait. The New York Mets picked him with the fourteenth selection in the 1961 expansion draft.

Hodges hit nine home runs for the 1962 Biggest Losers of All Time team and was a brief teammate of former Brooklyn slugging sidekick Duke Snider at the outset of the '63 season. The Mets dealt Hodges to Washington in May so he could be the Senators' manager.

The first baseman won a Gold Glove the first year of the award (1957), when one player was honored for each position in the majors, not in each league as is now the case.

There has been ongoing debate whether Hodges was Hall of Fame material. In addition to being, according to many, the best fielding first baseman ever, he hit 361 home runs with the Dodgers, driving in more than 100 runs seven years in a row.

His numbers are comparable to those of Johnny Mize, another first baseman, who is a Hall of Fame member. Mize hit 359 homers and had 1,337 RBIs, batting .312 over 15 years, while playing in five World Series. Hodges hit 370 homers with 1,274 RBIs batting .273 over 18 years, playing in seven World Series.

Pretty close, wouldn't you say?

Snider put together some truly astounding seasons, in terms of both production and consistency. At different times, he led he National League in runs, hits, home runs, RBIs, bases on balls, on-base percentage, and slugging percentage.

Five consecutive 40-plus home run years, an average of 108 runs batted in for a nine-year period, league-leading runs scored totals three years in a row, and six top-10 finishes in MVP voting. And 11 homers and 26 RBIs in six World Series.

The Duke, though he never had the flash and dazzle of the other two center fielders, belongs right there with Willie and Mickey, just as the song implies.

Snider placed placed third, fourth and second, respectively in National League MVP balloting from 1953–55. Campanella edged him by five points in '55, though each man received eight first-place votes.

Campy batted .318 that year, with 32 homers, 107 RBIs, 81 runs, 56 walks, and a .398 on-base percentage. Snider batted .309, with 42 homers, 136 RBIs, 126 runs, 104 walks, and a .418 on-base percentage. Campanella's leadership behind the plate almost surely was the deciding factor.

Just before the 1963 season, the Dodgers sold Snider to the Mets, reuniting him with his old Bums buddy, Hodges. Snider hit 14 home runs, was sold to San Francisco in April of '64, and ended his career with the Giants that season.

Furillo, a strong-throwing right fielder (151 lifetime assists), drove in 106 runs in back-to-back seasons, won the 1953 National League batting title with a .344 average, and hit 192 home runs over a 15-year career.

Having appeared in seven World Series, he played 10 games for the Dodgers in 1960 before they released him in May. Furillo's lifetime batting average was .299.

Sandy Amoros, a .255 lifetime hitter, grabbed the spotlight in the seventh game of the 1955 World Series. The Dodgers led the Yankees, 2–0. New York was threatening in the bottom of the sixth inning with two on, no outs, and Yogi Berra at the plate.

Berra sliced a drive toward the left-field corner, and Amoros, stationed in left-center, ran the ball down, then threw to shortstop Reese, who relayed to first base for a double play.

The catch was a game-saver as Brooklyn held on to take its first-ever World Series from the Yankees. Amoros, who had three good seasons for the Dodgers in the mid-'50s, did not hit above .200 after 1957. His career ended with Detroit in 1960 at the age of 30.

Jim Gilliam was not a utility man; he was an everyday player versatile enough to start at three positions. Mostly second base and third, with more than an occasional stint in left field.

Known as Junior, he set a lot of tables for the Dodgers in Brooklyn and Los Angeles. The leadoff man much of his career, he then batted behind Maury Wills and was the ideal number two hitter for a premier base stealer.

Gilliam had 17 triples, 100 walks, and 125 runs scored as the 1953 National League Rookie of the Year. The switch-hitter reached base nearly 3,000 times (36 percent of the time) in his 14-year-career, all with the Dodgers, while striking out only 416 times in more than 8,000 plate appearances.

He played fewer than 111 games (88) for the first time in 1966 and was released following the season. Gilliam appeared in seven World Series, helping the Dodgers win four of them.

Podres did not have one of his better years in 1955. Until the end. He pitched a shutout in the seventh game of the World Series to give the Dodgers their first Series championship vs. the Yankees.

Podres won twice in that Fall Classic and had a 4–1 lifetime Series record, helping the L.A. Dodgers win world titles in 1959 and '63.

After going 9–10 during regular season in '55, Podres spent a year in the military, then won 100 games from 1957–63. The southpaw's best season was 1961 when he went 18–5. In '63, five of his 14 victories were shutouts.

Podres was traded to Detroit in 1966 and was released by the Tigers after the '67 season. He did not pitch the next year, then signed with San Diego in 1969, where he closed out a 148-win career on July 21.

Carl Erskine (29), Billy Loes (19), lefty Karl Spooner, Russ Meyer (11), and Roger Craig (10) all made starts on the mound for the 1955 Dodgers.

That was Spooner's final season. Erskine, an 11-game winner in 1955, was done in '59, when he pitched 23 and a third innings for Los Angeles. Loes, who won 10 games for the '55 Dodgers, was traded to Baltimore the next year, and finished with the Giants in 1961. Meyer, a six-game winner for the 1955 Dodgers, was swapped to the Chicago Cubs following the season, and pitched for three additional teams, ending in '59 with the Kansas City Athletics.

Roger Craig's reputation for teaching the split-fingered fastball has overshadowed a pretty solid pitching career. The right-hander made 10 starts and won five of them for the 1955 Dodgers, won 12 for the '56 pennant-winning Brooklyns, and 11 for them when they took the 1959 flag.

He lost 46 games in the Mets' first two years, then had seven wins and five saves to help the Cardinals win the '64 pennant. He beat the Yankees in the World Series in 1955 and 1964, contributing to championships for Brooklyn and St. Louis, respectively.

It should be noted that Sandy Koufax was a rookie in 1955. He started five games for Brooklyn, going 2–2, with a 3.02. Both wins were complete-game shutouts. He did not pitch in the World Series.

The last former Brooklyn Dodger to play in a big league game was John Roseboro. He was Campanella's backup in 1957, the Dodgers' last year in Brooklyn.

Roseboro was the Dodgers' catcher their first 10 years in Los Angeles, playing in five World Series, three of which were victorious. He was traded to Minnesota and played two years with the Twins, who released him after the 1969 season.

Washington signed him. He had 86 at-bats for the Senators, the final one as a pinch-hitter on August 11, 1970, when he grounded out in a win over the Twins. Roseboro was released on August 19.

Yankees Crash and Burn

The New York Yankees' tumble was earth-shaking news. Of Richter Scale proportions in the baseball world. Without a doubt, one of the boldest sports headlines of the 1960s.

Making the Pinstripes' plummet more appalling was the fact that it was so dramatic. Not a mere fall, but an elevator crash from the fiftieth floor. In just one year, they went from the World Series, which they lost in seven games, to non-contender.

In the sixteen years prior to 1965, the Yankees had won fourteen American League pennants, while finishing second the other two times. They dropped all the way to sixth in 1965, 25 games behind pennant winner Minnesota, then plunged to last place in '66.

While New York's 1966 tenth-place finish was its lowest standings-wise (70–89, 26.5 games behind American League champion Baltimore), the Yanks' most distant ending was in 1969 when their 80–81 record left them 28.5 games back of the AL East Division champ Orioles. The Pinstripes had literally gone from the penthouse to the outhouse.

The Yankees' dominance is legendary. In the 44-year period from 1921, when they won their first league title, through 1964, the Yanks won 29 pennants and 20 World Series championships. They finished in second place eight times, third place five, fourth once, and seventh once.

That seventh, with a 69–85 record in 1925, marked the only time New York finished below .500 in that stretch of 44 years. Once in 44 seasons losing more than it won. Unbelievable!

So it was understandable that the Yankees' 1965slide was shocking. Not so much, however, when searching for the reasons why. One need look no farther than the roster.

The Yankees had grown very old, and they had very little talent on the farm. They were no longer the Bronx Bombers.

In 1964, CBS (the Columbia Broadcasting System) paid over 11 million dollars to buy 80 percent of the New York Yankees' stock from Del Webb and Dan Topping.

CBS soon found out that running television programming and a professional sports team were very different operations. The network was a failure in managing the Yankees.

During CBS's ownership, the team that had dominated major league baseball finished as high as second in the standings just once. Yankee Stadium attendance dropped below a million for a season for the first time since 1945.

In January of 1973, George Steinbrenner was announced as the owner of the New York Yankees.

In 1965, the star of the team was a pitcher. And his name wasn't Whitey Ford. **Mel Stottlemyre** was a 20-game winner. Ford, 36 years old, won 16 but lost 13. Tom Tresh was the only Yankee to hit as many as 20 home runs (26), and his .279 batting average and 74 runs batted in also led the club. Mickey Mantle hit 19 homers and drove in 46. Roger Maris mustered eight and 27 in 155 at-bats.

In 1966, **Joe Pepitone** was the Yankees' biggest bopper with 31 home runs and 83 RBIs. Mantle's figures were .288–23–56 in 333 at-bats; Maris' .233–13–43 in 348. Stottlemyre was a 20-game loser. Ford pitched just 73 innings.

In 1967, **Horace Clarke's** .272 average topped New York, with Mantle third at .245, along with 55 RBIs and a team-high 22 home runs. Maris was gone, traded to St. Louis in the off season. The club's 522 runs scored were the fewest in the American League, a good explanation for its 72–90 record and ninth-place finish.

In 1968, things were looking up as the Yankees climbed back over .500, improving to 83–79. They remained far out of the race, however, and ended in fifth place, 20 games behind AL winner Detroit. Roy White led New York in hitting at .267 and RBIs with 62. Mantle's 18 homers were tops on the team. Stottlemyre won 21 games. Former Cleveland and Detroit slugger Rocky Colavito pitched two and two-thirds scoreless innings and picked up a victory.

In 1969, the Yanks slipped back under .500, their 80–81 record landing them in fifth place in the six-team AL East division and seventh overall. White hit .290, Pepitone had 27 homers, and **Bobby Murcer** knocked in 82, all team highs. Stottlemyre won 20 for the third time in the '60s.

Nothing may have symbolized the futility of the Yankees in the second half of the decade more than Tom Tresh's disappointing descent.

Yankees faithful could not help but compare Tresh to Mantle when the former joined the club. They certainly hoped for a reincarnation.

Like Mantle, Tresh was a switch-hitter and came up as a shortstop. He stirred those hopes with a Rookie-of-the-Year 1962 season, batting .286 with 20 home runs and 93 RBIs.

When Tony Kubek was discharged from the military in August, he took over at short for New York and Tresh went to the outfield. He remained there over the next five seasons before being moved back to shortstop.

Tresh's first season would be his best all-around. He never again batted as high as .280 and never again drove in more than 74 runs. He did bang 25, 26, and 27 homers but also had 11, 14, and 16.

His production declined markedly when he was 28, and his career was over two years later. After hitting .195 in 1968 and starting '69 at .211 with one home run in 45 games, Tresh was traded to Detroit where he ended the year and his career. He was finished at the age of 30.

Mantle's Exit More Bitter Than Sweet

There were better baseball players than Mickey Mantle. It is doubtful there have been any who were more popular or more glamorous.

The Mick was one of a handful whose arrival in the batter's box made everyone in the ballpark stop everything and watch him. The atmosphere was electric because he was capable of the miraculous.

The dictionary's synonyms for glamorous include beautiful, bewitching, beguiling, charismatic, appealing, alluring, thrilling, and stimulating.

Mantle was all of those adjectives, and more, in the eyes of New York Yankees fans and—other than ardent Yankee haters—in the eyes of baseball fans everywhere.

He had the name. He had the game. A switch-hitter with massive power from both sides of the plate, he possessed amazing speed that was particularly evident running from home to first base, going from first to third, and turning apparent extra-base hits into outs in center field.

Mantle astounded folks. By launching mammoth home runs worthy of joining the solar system. With a drag bunt that he patented, taking the ball with him from the left side of the plate and racing to first before the second baseman could make a play.

Sometimes he did both in the same game, inspiring a shaking of heads from dugouts to bleachers. Country-boy good looks and a bashful grin added to the All-American image. He could do it all.

At times, Mantle did do it all. Like 1956, when he won the American League triple crown, batting .353 with 52 home runs and 130 runs batted in, while also leading the league in runs scored with 132, a .705 slugging percentage, and 376 total bases.

He hit .365 and had a .512 on-base percentage the very next season, slammed 54 homers in 1961, and scored more than 100 runs nine years in a row.

Mantle even cut a record with singing star Teresa Brewer.

His last big year came in 1964 when he was only 32 — 35–111–.303 — as he failed to hit more than 23 homers or drive in more than 56 runs his final four seasons.

Mantle came through on the big stage, hitting 18 home runs and knocking in 40 runs in 65 World Series games, helping the Yankees win seven of the dozen Fall Classics in which he played.

His last time at bat came on September 28, 1968 — eight years to the day and in Fenway Park, the same place Williams had homered in his final at-bat. Mantle was listed as the Yankees' first baseman that day, but he never took the field.

His right knee and ankle were sore, and it was manager Ralph Houk's plan to let Mantle bat and then remove him from the game. He popped out to Boston shortstop Rico Petrocelli in short left field in the first inning and then was replaced by Andy Kosco.

Mantle finished with a .298 lifetime batting average. What had looked like a sure .300 career mark was dragged down by three miserable seasons over his last four. In 1965, '67, and '68, he combined to bat .245, dipping to .237 in 1968.

He was 36 when he quit and probably stuck around too long.

Chance of a Lifetime

Dean Chance was the real deal. Noted probably too much for being **Bo Belinsky's** play pal and not enough as the outstanding pitcher he was, the right-hander carved out some accomplishments that rivaled the best hurlers of his time.

Sadly, his time was too short. After winning 110 games in seven seasons by the age of 27, Chance managed only 18 more victories in a career that was over when he was 30. A back injury and the innings overload were mentioned as possible reasons for his early demise.

He won 14 games with a 2.92 earned run average in his first full season in the majors, one that began when Chance was 20 years old.

Two years later, in 1964, he produced glossy numbers that included a 20–9 record, 11 shutouts, and a 1.65 over 278 innings, with just 194 hits allowed.

Chance was rewarded with the Cy Young Award. Emphasis on THE as there was only one such award for the entire major leagues until 1967, the first year a pitcher was anointed in both the National and American League.

Chance won 20 again in 1967, his first season with the Minnesota Twins after spending five years (74 wins) with the Los Angeles Angels. In '68, he went 16–16, his 2.53 ERA worthy of a much better record. But the Twins scored two or fewer runs in 17 of his starts.

He pitched 206, 248, 278, 225, 259, 283, and 292 innings from 1962–68, never allowing as many hits in a season as the number of innings he worked.

That is one of two shining statistics on his career work log: 1,864 hits given up in 2,147 and a third innings pitched. The other is his 2.92 ERA.

MLB Implements the Draft

Major League Baseball's first amateur draft was held June 8, 1965, at the Commodore Hotel in New York City.

The Kansas City Athletics made outfielder Rick Monday, a sophomore at Arizona State University, the number one pick. The first draft lasted two days, with 813 players selected.

Teams picked in reverse order of their finish from the previous season, with the major league team with the worst record going first and the team with the best record going last.

Previously, every major league team was eligible to sign any amateur player. This promoted the old saying that the rich get richer. Teams with the most money signed more of the outstanding prospects, which helped them achieve repeated success and bring in more money, thus continuing the cycle.

Among other big-name players selected in that first draft were Tom Seaver, Johnny Bench, and Nolan Ryan. Bench signed with Cincinnati and Ryan signed with the New York Mets, while Seaver, chosen by the Los Angeles Dodgers, returned to Southern Cal to continue his college career.

The draft has been held every year since its inception.

Postscript

The Baltimore Orioles won the most games of all major league teams in the 1960s, 911, an average of 91 victories per season. The San Francisco Giants were close behind with 902, followed by the New York Yankees with 887.

The Yanks, as has been documented here, were pretty much two teams during the decade, a different one for each five-year period. New York appeared in the first five World Series of the '60s, winning two and losing three, then disappeared from contention.

The Dodgers and Cardinals both played in three Series during the decade, each going 2–1, while Baltimore and Detroit both split in their two 1960s Fall Classics.

The Orioles, after losing to the Mets in the '69 World Series, continued to be a force entering the next decade. The Birds won the 1970 World Championship and lost in seven games in '71. Three straight Series and four in six years is pretty awesome.

So was Harmon Killebrew's monstrous power display. The Killer opened the 1970s by eclipsing the 40 mark in home runs for an astonishing eighth time.

Hank Aaron, second to the Twins' slugger in '60s homers, showed his prowess if not his age. The Hammer slugged 159 home runs in the first four years of the new decade, carrying him through age 39.

The 1960s leading hit maker, Roberto Clemente, just kept them coming as long as he was alive—.352, .341, and .312 to ring in the 1970s.

Numbers, big ones like 3,000 and 715, would be added to the splendid lore of a splendid game. The record-breaking is always going to happen.

But for sheer mystique and magic, it will always be hard to match those Mazzin', Yazzin', Amazin' 1960s.

Bibliography

BOOKS

Groat, Dick, and Surface, Bill. *The World Champion Pittsburgh Pirates*. New York, NY: Coward-McCann, Inc., 1961.

Kahn, Roger. *The Era*. New York, NY: Ticknor & Fields, Houghton Mifflin Company, 1993.

Morales, Bill. *Farewell to the Last Golden Era*. Jefferson, NC: McFarland and Company, Inc., Publishers, 2011.

Nowlin, Bill, and Stahl, John Harry. *Drama and Pride in the Gateway City – The 1964 St. Louis Cardinals*. Lincoln, NE: University of Nebraska Press and the Society for American Baseball Research, 2013.

Peary, Danny. *We Played the Game*. New York, NY: Hyperion, 1994.

Solomon, Burt. *The Baseball Timeline*. New York, NY: DK Publishing, Inc., 2001.

WEBSITES
Baseball-almanac.com

Baseball-Reference.com

MLB.com

SABR.org

Thisgreatgame.com/1960s-baseball-history.html

INTERVIEWS

(in-person)

    Roberto Clemente

(telephone)

    Tom Seaver

    George Altman

    Dick Groat

    Tony Cloninger

    Dick Schofield

    Bob Friend

Player Index